BASICS

FASHION DESIGN

01

RESEARCH
AND DESIGN

2nd edition

Fairchild Books
An imprint of Bloomsbury Publishing Plc

B L O O M S B U R Y
LONDON · NEW DELHI · NEW YORK · SYDNEY

Fairchild Books
An imprint of Bloomsbury Publishing Plc

Imprint previously known as AVA Publishing

50 Bedford Square
London
WC1B 3DP
UK

1385 Broadway
New York
NY 10018
USA

www.bloomsbury.com

**FAIRCHILD BOOKS, BLOOMSBURY and the Diana logo are trademarks of
Bloomsbury Publishing Plc**

First published in 2007 by AVA Publishing
Reprinted by AVA Publishing in 2012
Reprinted by Fairchild Books in 2014, 2015

© Bloomsbury Publishing Plc, 2012

British Library Cataloguing-in-Publication Data
A catalogue record for this book is available from the British Library.

ISBN: PB: 978-2-9404-1170-2
ePDF: 978-2-9404-4730-5

Library of Congress Cataloging-in-Publication Data

Seivewright, Simon.
Basics Fashion Design 01: Research and Design/
Simon Seivewright
p. cm.
Includes bibliographical references and index.
ISBN 9782940411702 (pbk.: alk.paper)
eISBN 9782940447305
1. Fashion design. 2. Fashion design–Study and teaching.
TT507 .S358 2011

Cover illustration by Tacita Meredith.
Design by John F McGill.
Printed and bound in China

0.1 |
○ **Viktor and Rolf SS11.**
Catwalking.com

Contents

Introduction

Research and design

Research is vital to any design process as it will provide you with the foundations with which to build and develop your desired creative outcomes. Research involves the initial trawl and collection of ideas prior to design. It should be an experimental process; an investigation to find out or support your knowledge of a particular subject, market, consumer, innovation or technology.

Research is an essential tool in the creative process and is one that will provide you with information and creative direction, as well as a narrative to a collection. Research is about a journey of discovery that can often take weeks or even months to collate and process. It is also a very personal activity, which provides the viewer with an insight into the thinking, aspirations, interests and creative vision of the designer.

By conducting in-depth and broad-ranging research, a designer can begin to interpret a series of garments or to evolve a collection. Silhouettes, textures and fabrics, colours, details, print and embellishment, and market and consumer will all have their place in the process of design and will all be found or directed by the research gathered.

This new edition of *Basics Fashion Design: Research and Design* will lead you through the essential stages of research and the translation of these into fashion design ideas. It will discuss crucial elements in the research and design process, such as the brief and the constraints that this can sometimes impose. It will explain the importance of identifying both your target market and customer, and of understanding the different levels and genres of fashion before setting out on the creative research itself. It will then discuss the many possible avenues for research and the need to set a theme, concept or narrative to your collection.

'I get my ideas out of my dreams… if you're lucky enough to use something you see in a dream, it is purely original. It's not in the world – it's in your head. I think that is amazing.'
Alexander McQueen
British fashion designer
1969–2010

How you translate your research into early design ideas is then explored, looking at both 2D and 3D approaches, and useful exercises are provided for you to do which explain how to bridge the gap between the research and design outcomes. Design and collection development is broken down into a series of elements that then provide a foundation for expanding your ideas into a well-considered, cohesive and balanced collection. Finally, the book shows and explores a variety of approaches to communicating and rendering your design work.

Interviews at the end of each chapter, featuring established international fashion designers, a trend forecasting agency, a fashion illustrator and fashion students will inspire you on your creative journey throughout the book, and will provide you with valuable insights into what it means to get into, work in and succeed within the fashion industry.

Research and Design will provide you with the fundamental skills and knowledge that you need to start you on your journey of designing an in-depth, innovative and creative collection all of your own. Good luck – and above all, enjoy the discovery of the creative design process!

◑ **Alexander McQueen pheasant-inspired dress detail S/S11.**
Catwalking.com

Introduction

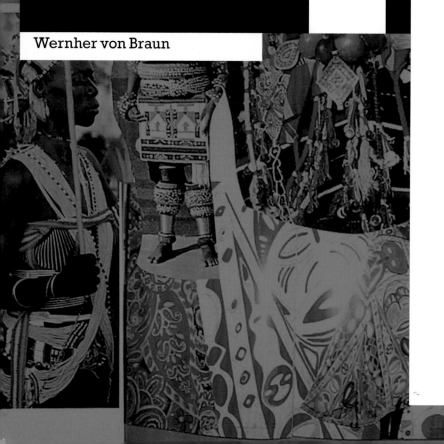

Research <small>is what I'm</small>
doing <small>when</small> I don't know
<small>what</small> I'm doing.

Wernher von Braun

Research is about creative investigation, and
it is about recording information for use now
or in the future. But what exactly is research?
Designers are constantly looking for new ideas,
as fashion by its very nature is always changing
and reinventing itself. But where does it all start?

In this first chapter, we aim to demystify what
research is, as well as to explore the creative
investigation process a little further. We will also
look at why you should research in the first place.
The chapter discusses what a brief is, the different
types of brief that exist and what it is that the
designer is being asked to do.

What do you need to consider as a designer
before you begin work on any project or
collection? This is a question that every designer
should ask themselves. Later on in the chapter,
we will explore what the purpose of research
is and what precisely it should contain in terms
of information.

Above all, the process of research should be
fun, exciting, informative and (most importantly)
useful. This chapter will help you to discover
how you can make it all of these things!

The brief is usually the start to any creative project and the project is a sustained body of work that is normally time-bound. The purpose of a brief is essentially to inspire you and to outline the aims and objectives that are required. It will identify any constraints, conditions or problems that need to be solved, as well as providing you with information on what final outcomes or tasks are to be achieved. The brief is there to help you and more importantly to guide the whole research and design process.

Types of brief

There are several types of brief. The most common one is found within the academic forum where it is usually set by the tutor and asks you as an individual to respond to it. The aims are what you are expected to learn and the objectives will be the work demonstrated. As the student, you will be expected to answer not only the brief's creative requirements, but also the assessment criteria that will be clearly identified. The brief is used as an important tool by the tutor to help teach specific skills and develop and improve your knowledge and understanding.

A further type of brief also found within the academic forum is one for a competition often set by a company or external organization as a way of promoting products or a brand and in turn, encouraging new talent within the industry. This association with industry will often provide sponsorship, placement awards and travel bursaries for the students taking part.

Commercial and client-based are the other types of briefs you will come across as a designer. These will have very specific aims and objectives that will consider some or all of the following: market, season, genres, cost and occasion. The true measure of your creativity as a designer will be to achieve something exciting and innovative while considering very closely what it is that you are being asked to produce and adhering to the constraints of the brief in order to achieve the client's approval.

Another common type of brief is one that asks you to work within a team, for example, a large high-street brand. Here you will be expected to work with others on a project and you will have specific tasks assigned to you that will ultimately work towards presenting a coherent and cohesive collection.

Working to a commercial brief

A good example of a designer working to a commercial brief is supplied by British designer Julien Macdonald, who redesigned the British Airways uniform. Here the brief would have had very specific criteria and restrictions on design, use of fabric, cost, function and performance.

What was the brief British Airways set you?

I was asked along with many other designers to come up with a set of sketches for uniforms that could be worn by all the different British Airways staff from all over the world. The uniforms had to be functional pieces that could be worn by the cabin crew to the ground staff to the baggage handlers, over 80,000 employees worldwide.

The designs were submitted anonymously to the British Airways board of directors and design team so that the ideas would not be judged on the name of the designer. They were really surprised when they found out that the clean, simple, stylish ideas were mine, as they associated my name with glitz and glamour!

What constraints did you face?

There were many complex constraints as the investment by the company was worth millions of pounds and the last time it was changed was over ten years ago, when Paul Costelloe did the designs. The clothes had to fit from a size 6 to 22, be for both men and women, and there was to be no discrimination between race, colour or creed. The garments had to be in the same fabric, whether you were working in a Russian winter or the summer in the Seychelles.

I spent time working alongside the staff to find out about their working lives – from leaving their homes to going to work to then arriving in a hotel after a ten-hour flight and having to wash the blouse in the sink to have it fresh for the return flight the next morning! The garments were given a pilot period where we looked at how they performed under normal working conditions. For example, did the fabric wear well? Did the buttons fall off? The final garments were then successfully put into production and can be seen on any current flight with British Airways.

Read the full interview with Julien Macdonald on pages 148–151.

What's in a brief?

Occasion and season

As a designer, it is important to be aware of whether you are designing for a specific occasion or season, which will have an impact on many of the design factors, such as fabric and colour.

Muse or customer

A brief will sometimes ask you to design for a very specific consumer of a certain age, size and gender. It may also ask you to build a customer profile and to consider elements such as background, work, lifestyle and income.

Target market

A brief will often ask you to focus on a specific market sector in the industry, such as high street or middle-market price points. This again requires you to consider market analysis and customer profiling.

Material and fabric

Sometimes in the academic field you will be asked to problem solve a brief that focuses your creativity on the use of a particular type or quality of fabric, for example, jersey.

Costing

Most project briefs, whether they are academic or industry set, will require you to consider the price that something will cost.

Practical outcomes

These are simply what you are expected to produce. The brief may have a specific garment type as its final outcome – a dress, a jacket, or a piece of knitwear, for example.

Fashion by its very definition is about current popular custom or style; the fashion designer expresses the zeitgeist, or spirit of the times in their work. Fashion is constantly changing and the designer is expected to recreate the wheel every season. Because of this constant pressure for the new, designers have to dig ever deeper and search ever further for new inspiration and ways of interpreting this into their collections. Fashion designers are therefore like magpies – obsessive collectors always on the hunt for new and exciting things to inspire them. So the need to gather and source material for use in the creative process is essential for feeding the imagination.

Three types of research

Research is about investigation; learning about something new or learning about something from the past. It can often be likened to the beginning of a journey of exploration. It is about reading, visiting or perhaps viewing, but above all, it is about recording information.

There are three types of research. The first type is the visual inspiration for the collection, and this will often help to set the theme, mood or concept that is essential in developing an identity for your creative work. The second is gathering and sourcing the tangible and practical materials for your collection – for example, fabric, trims and buttons. The third is perhaps the most important aspect as it relates to the consumer and market that you are creating the design work for. The brief may already state the market, but as a designer it is essential that you explore and identify who you are designing for and understand their lifestyle and interests, as well as researching the broader market and competitors within it.

Undertaking all three aspects of research will give you a much more solid foundation upon which to build your design ideas. Your research should always be broad-ranging and in-depth, enabling you to innovate, rather than to simply imitate in the collection that you create from it.

Research could be likened to a diary or journal, a snapshot of who you are, what you are interested in and what is happening in the world at a specific time. Trends, along with social and political issues, could be documented as part of your research – as all these things have an impact on the research and creative design process. The information compiled in your research diary is likely to be useful both now and in the future.

Research – what and why?

> 'Research is formalized curiosity. It is poking and prying with a purpose.'
> Zora Neale Hurston
> American folklorist
> and writer, 1891–1960

What is the purpose of research?

We know what research is, but why do we need it? How does it help you as a designer?

Research is there, above all, to inspire you as a creative individual. It is a way of stimulating the mind and opening up new directions in design. By gathering different references and exploring many avenues of interest, you can begin to explore a variety of creative possibilities before you channel and focus your imagination towards a concept, theme or direction for a collection.

Research will help you to learn about a subject. You might discover information previously unknown to you, or perhaps new skills or technologies could be explored.

Research is an opportunity to inquire into your own interests and expand your awareness and knowledge of the world around you. As a result, research is very much a personal and individual task, and although a team of people can gather it, one person generally has the creative vision and takes the lead.

Research is a way of showing the world how you see it and how you think. And this is extremely important in differentiating you from everyone else in the industry. Think of it as a personal diary of a moment in your creative lifetime and a document to show whoever is interested what has inspired you and had an effect on your life.

The final thing to remember is that research must above all else be inspiring and useful.

○ Example of student research and early inspirational ideas.

As we have already discovered, research is about the investigation and recording of information. This information can be usefully broken down into a series of categories that will help to inspire you, as well as providing the different components of a collection's direction.

Crinoline

This is a lightweight frame constructed by connecting horizontal hoops of wire and cotton tape together. Crinolines were worn under skirts to allow the silhouette of the body to be exaggerated. Their use was at its most popular and extreme in shape during the mid-to-late 1800s.

Shapes and structures

By its very definition, 'shape' is an area or form with a definite outline and a visible appearance and structure. It is also the way in which something is constructed or supported in a framework. Shapes are a vital element of research and ultimately of design too, as they provide you with potential ideas to translate onto the body and into garments. Without shape, there would be no silhouettes in fashion design (see pages 118–120).

To support shape, it is also important to consider structure and how something is constructed or created. The potential to understand how a framework or parts can support shape is vital and again this can be translated into fashion design. Consider the role of a domed roof of a cathedral, contemporary glasshouse or the crinoline frame of a nineteenth-century dress, for example.

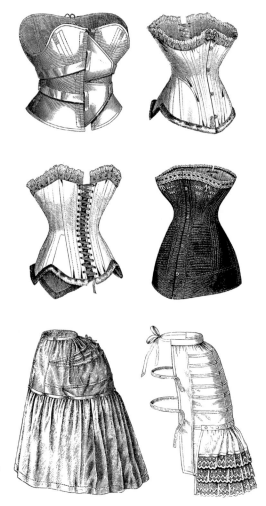

○ **Historical examples of nineteenth-century crinolines and corsets used to exaggerate the human silhouette.**
Dover Press

Research – what and why?

○ **Example of a student sketchbook clearly demonstrating the influence of architecture on garment design.**

○ **Reichstag Building, Germany. The internal structure shown in this image links closely with that of a nineteenth-century crinoline.**
Photographer: Nigel Young.
Courtesy of Nigel Young/
Foster + Partners.

Details

As a designer, it is important that you not only consider inspiration for shape in your research, but also for the more practical elements like the details. The details of a garment can be anything from where the topstitching is placed to pocket types, fastenings, and shapes of cuffs and collars. The details of a garment are equally important to design as is the silhouette, as these will often be the main selling feature once it is given closer examination by buyers. It is therefore essential that you incorporate detailing in order to create a successful and more evolved garment.

The research gathered for this element of the design process can come from many different sources. It may be that you explore the pockets and cuffs of a military jacket or take elements from an historical garment. It may be that the details come from a more abstract source, for example, a pocket shape may be inspired by something more organic. The inspiration for the detailing on a garment, or a whole collection, should filter through from all the different sources that you have researched. The detailing may not be immediately obvious, but as you will learn, it is an important part of the design process and must ultimately be considered.

◐◑ Irish Guards' military dress jacket.

◑ Sheepskin collar detail on men's DSquared flight jacket.

⚬ **Cropped trenchcoat-inspired jacket with stud detailing. Burberry S/S11.**
Catwalking.com

Topstitching

This is any stitching visible on the right side of a garment. It can be decorative, but its main function is to reinforce a seam. It can commonly be seen in denim garments such as jeans.

◐◑ **A selection of colour-themed inspiration boards.**

Colour

Colour is a fundamental consideration in the research and design process. It is often the first element that is noticed about a design and influences how that garment or collection is perceived. Colour has fascinated us since ancient times and in our clothing it reflects personality, character and taste, and can also convey significant messages reflecting different cultures and social status.

As a designer, colour is often the starting point of a collection and can control the mood and season that you are designing for. The research you gather for colour should be both primary and secondary, and allow you to mix and play with a variety of combinations.

Where your inspiration comes from is limitless as we live in a world surrounded by colour. Nature, for instance, provides you with an unlimited array of colours, shades and tones that can be translated into a palette for the design process. However, your inspiration could equally come from an artist or a specific painting or period in history.

Palette

This is a piece of board that an artist mixes up paint on before painting, but as a designer it means a group of colours that are mixed together. They can coordinate, have similar hues and tones or can be juxtaposed and clash.

In chapter four, we will discuss colour theory and the use of colour palettes in the design of a collection.

What is research? > What should research contain? > Who are you designing for?

Textures

Texture refers to the surface quality of objects and appeals to our sense of touch. Light and dark patterns of different textures can provide visual stimulation for the viewer without them actually having to touch an object, as well as describing the surface that is presented.

As a fashion designer, research into texture will ultimately lead to fabric and the many different qualities and finishes available to you (see pages 128–133). The way that something looks and feels on the body is a crucial part of the design process, but inspiration for this can come from many different sources.

The textures you research can often inspire new ideas for surface manipulation and the way that a fabric handles will help to define and possibly shape a garment. Images of building materials, landscapes and organic forms may help to inspire knitwear and fabric manipulation techniques, such as pleating.

○ **Sophia Kokosalaki S/S06 dress inspired by shell-like textures and patterns.**
Catwalking.com

○ **Ernst Haeckel's illustration of seashells explores art forms in nature.**
Dover Press

O Research board inspired
by African decorative costume.

Print and surface decoration

Through the process of research, you may well start to gather information and references that have natural patterns or decorations on them and which lend themselves to be interpreted into print and textile development. Images or objects may well be decorative, jewelled, repeated, mirrored or provide an opportunity for a motif within a design concept.

Surface qualities may also suggest translation into textile techniques, such as embroidery, smocking, appliqué and beading (see pages 172–173). Surface finishes can be applied to a fabric or garment to alter the look, feel and perhaps reflect the mood of the source of inspiration. For example, distressed, aged and faded might be translated from scorched arid land in Africa; or jewelled and decorative qualities could be translated from sourced Indian sari fabrics.

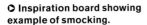

○ Inspiration board showing
example of smocking.

○ African-inspired beaded
bomber jacket. Joe Goode
menswear AW11.

Cultural influences

Cultural influences can be everything from the appreciation of literature, arts and music from your own country to the appreciation of the customs and civilization of another. Looking at another country for ideas can provide you with a wealth of inspiration that may translate itself into colour, fabric, and print and garment shapes. Designers such as John Galliano and Jean Paul Gaultier are well known for the way they look to many different cultures as a springboard for their collections.

As a designer, you may be inspired by literature and employ this to provide a narrative to your collection; current art exhibitions in museums and galleries may also have an influence on the research that you gather and the creations you design.

**◐◑ Jean Paul Gaultier
S/S98 and A/W05,
Frida Kahlo-inspired and
Mexican-inspired collections.**
Catwalking.com

○ Christian Dior haute
couture S/S07. Designed by
John Galliano, inspired by
Japanese costume.
Catwalking.com

○ Japanese scene created
by the master Kunisada,
circa 1845.

What is research? > What should research contain? > Who are you designing for?

'It was interesting to explore historical clothes and to think about those textures, those embroideries, those materials and then to interpret them for a woman today, not as costume, but as wardrobe.'
Nicolas Ghesquière at Balenciaga

Historical influences

As with working in any creative field, it is essential to have an understanding of what has taken place in the past in order to move ideas and technologies forward. Historical influences may be found in any design discipline from any culture. They could be as diverse as looking at ancient tiles from an Islamic mosque to Japanese samurai armour.

A key element of historical research must be that of dress history or costume. Learning about dress history is an extremely important part of being a fashion designer and for many it has provided a treasure trove and wealth of information on everything from shape and tailoring to fabric and embellishment.

Vivienne Westwood describes the process of looking at historical dress for inspiration as 'synthesizing the old into the new'. She is certainly famous for exploring many different centuries of costume to invigorate her collections. Fashion by its definition is about current popular trends and so looking at costume provides you with an insight into trends of that period.

⟲ **Triple portrait of Charles I by Anthony van Dyck (1599–1641) showing the distinctive lace collars of the baroque period.**

⟲ **Givenchy haute couture A/W98. Designed by Alexander McQueen and inspired by Anthony van Dyck.**
Catwalking.com

Contemporary trends

Having an awareness of events and cultural trends is something that you must develop as a designer. Observing global changes, social trends and political climates is essential in creating clothes for a specific target market. Tracking trends is not necessarily a fully conscious activity, but merely an ability to tune in to the spirit of the times or zeitgeist. It also requires an awareness of subtle changes in taste and interests that often start out on the 'street'.

The 'bubble-up effect' describes how activities, special interests and subcultural groups have an influence on mainstream culture – often through music and exposure on television – and are seen as a new direction for fashion and media.

Fashion forecasting agencies (see pages 146–147) and trend magazines (page 54) are just some of the ways in which you can easily gain access to this sort of information.

Tangible and material research

As well as considering potential sources of visual inspiration, it is also essential to gather ideas for the more tangible and material components of a collection.

As a fashion designer, you are considering how the body is to be covered, wrapped, protected, decorated and transformed, and therefore working with and understanding materials is an essential part of that process. Tangible research at this early stage can simply be about discovering objects and items such as new and old fabrics, or antique buttons and trims, such as lace. It might be that a vintage garment could inspire a textile manipulation, quality or surface decoration. On a cultural visit, you might have gathered artefacts that then inspire new variations and interpretations at a later stage.

It is these more tangible objects that can often help you to understand the use and function of them in the design of a garment, as well as to inspire you to develop ideas from them later on in the process.

○ **Selection of research material, from wallpaper designs to buttons, trims and sketchbook references.**

It is important to consider your market (the third aspect of research) as early as possible, as it will often dictate and define where you should begin. As already discussed in 'Types of brief' (see page 10), it may well be that an externally-set brief, provided by a client, company or your tutor, outlines any constraints or market levels that you should be considering in the research and design process. Having a solid understanding of the customer and the competitors you are facing at the start of the project means that you will have a more focused and well-targeted collection in the end.

○ Madonna in a publicity shot for Louis Vuitton in 2008.
© Getty images

Identifying your market

Early market research could simply involve looking at examples of the advertising and brand identity, online presence, store layouts and merchandise for a particular design, brand or company that you feel falls in line with the customer you would like to design for. Brands will often have a clear muse or model type that defines their ideal customer or will perhaps create one which consumers will aspire to, promoted with the message, 'if you dress in our garments, you too could look like this'.

This early market research could take the form of collected promotional material, such as look books, online images, magazine adverts, catwalk images, store photographs, window displays, packaging and logos, sketches of key garments, written information, company mission and target customer statements.

This type of material can be collected across a range of brands within a certain market level to enable you to understand how competitors differentiate between one another and create a signature identity to their brand and designs. This type of research activity can often be described as shop/brand reporting.

Identifying a muse

You may wish to identify a muse of your own at this early stage of the process, as this can often help with the focus of who is going to wear your clothes. Having a muse or specific customer in mind allows you to refer to this person when designing the collection. Would that person wear this garment? How and when would they wear it? Does it connect to and enhance that person and their own style or identity?

'She gave the most to fashion because of her beauty and personality… that marvellous face and those strong little shoulders.'
Hubert de Givenchy on Audrey Hepburn

Designers will often have a particular model, actress or singer that they feel epitomizes their brand – or at least they do for that season! Hubert de Givenchy famously worked with the actress Audrey Hepburn for many years, helping to create her iconic style. A good example today is provided by Madonna, who over the years has been connected to designer brands such as Jean Paul Gaultier, Dolce and Gabbana, Versace and, more recently, Louis Vuitton. Her strong personal identity and celebrity thereby become linked to that specific designer and the aspirations of the customer to purchase from that brand.

Later on, we will look more closely at the different market levels and genres within fashion so that you better understand the breadth of the industry and the market that is potentially available to you as a designer (pages 138–141).

Brainstorming

In this chapter, you have learnt about the importance of research and some of the key categories that it can fall into.

This exercise is designed to get you thinking laterally and broadly within the main research categories to develop possible avenues for visual, tangible and market research.

Use dictionaries, a thesaurus and the Internet to assist in this activity. Pictures can also be assigned to the words written down and therefore provide you with potential starting points for your collection and also possible ideas for a theme or concept.

Be open-minded and allow your imagination to wander into many different related and unrelated areas; the juxtaposition of words and themes can often present new concepts and marriages for the design.

Start by selecting one of the following visual research categories:

- shapes and structures
- details
- colour
- textures
- print and embellishment
- historical influences
- cultural influences
- contemporary trends.

Then think of something that might be connected or relate to that category, for example, red for the colour category, or China for the cultural category, or geometric for shapes and structures, or the 1920s for the history category.

Using this first subject or topic, begin to branch out as many ideas, words, meanings, descriptions, places and objects as you can. Make sure that you also start to add in references for the other research categories that may or may not relate to the first topic that you wrote down.

Remember: you can use a dictionary and a thesaurus to help with words and meanings to branch away from the first word listed.

As you begin to develop a series of words and directions, add in ideas for possible tangible elements, such as artefacts, trims or fabric types that could relate to and be sourced at the next stage. You could also start to think of people that could be associated with some of the ideas generated; these could be models, celebrities, actors, musicians or even figures from history or literature.

Danger
- Blood
- Stop
- Prohibited
- Warning
- Hazard --- Signs
- Red tape

Red stone
- Garnet
- Ruby
- Ayers Rock (Uluru), Australia

Organic
- Fruits
  - Berries --- Strawberries
  - Cherry --- Grapes
  - --- Wines
  - Chilli
  - Plum
  - Pepper
- Autumnal leaves
- Flowers
  - Petals
  - Red roses

Emotions
- Red light district
  - Desire --- Valentine
- Passion
  - Love --- Hatred
- Rage --- Anger
- Strength

Military
- 'British Redcoats' --- Napoleonic uniform --- Highland Regiment
- Musketeers --- 19th century --- Regency women's dress
- Britain --- Red, white and blue --- Buckingham Palace, guards
  - --- London

Tribal
- Aboriginal --- Eclectic cultures
- Mexican
  - Dance --- Oriental
- African
  - Salsa --- China
- Traditional dress
  - Flamenco --- Traditional dress
- Embellishment
  - Red – good luck
- Beads

Nature
- Insects --- Ladybirds
- Holly --- Festive
- Poppies
- Tulip

Rouge
Scarlet
Crimson
Burgundy
Cherry
Russet

Hot/Heat/Warmth
- Warm colour palette
- Spices --- Devil
- Fire, burn, flame --- Hell

Architecture
- Red brick
  - Clay --- Earthenware --- Pottery
  - Houses --- Rustic
  - Walls --- Pattern
- Rusted metal
  - Sculpture
  - Texture

Advertising
- Playing cards
  - Hearts
  - Diamonds
- Casino --- Dice
- Gambling --- Chips
- Corporate --- VIP
- Logos, slogans --- Red carpet

Alice Palmer

Alice Palmer has a background in textiles and graduated from Glasgow School of Art in 2000, and set up a business selling fashion accessories in 2001. With a passion for making garments, she moved to London to study for a Masters at the Royal College of Art (2005–7) and launched her knitwear label in 2008.

Based in London, she continues to develop unconventional ways of constructing knitwear. In 2008, she won the 'Best Womenswear Designer' award during New York Fashion Week and was also nominated for Designer of the Year at the Scottish Style Awards.

How do you start the research process?

I am constantly inspired by all of my surroundings, whether it be art, architecture, nature, science, people, films or the theatre – absolutely anything that can trigger ideas for colour, shape and form.

What kind of brief/constraints/ direction/market do you work to?

In approaching a collection, I might have a particular woman in mind who I would like to dress, which really helps me to visualize the finished garment and may help towards deciding on the overall look. My main focus always begins with developing innovative techniques within knitting, which then dictates the language of the collection.

Do you set themes? If so how and where do these start?

Occasionally I use themes, such as my Autumn/ Winter 2010 collection, 'Batman'. This came around when I was developing a three-dimensional knitting technique and the outcome reminded me of the Batmobile; Batman then became the basis of my collection for shape and form, and also influenced the colours I used and the studded details.

I believe themes can give cohesion to a collection, though there is also a danger that the theme could restrict you so that you end up designing for one particular type of person.

○ **Alice Palmer S/S11.**
Catwalking.com

○ **Alice Palmer's
studio research wall.**
Photographer: Sam Bailey

What are your sources of inspiration?

I am mainly inspired by visiting art galleries, such as the Schwartz Gallery in Hackney Wick, London, where I find inspiration in the installation art and sculpture. Museums such as the Natural History Museum and Science Museum in London, Japanese design for the innovation, modern architecture, art and films also provide inspiration. At the moment, I am particularly inspired by Gustav Mesmer, an eccentric inventor of non-powered flight machines, and by the British sculptor Anish Kapoor.

Do you have sources that you repeat or revisit in seasons or collections?

I am continually drawn towards Japanese architecture for the silhouette of my garments, to give a modern edge.

How important is the research to the design process?

I believe research is fundamental towards finding an initial direction. Even once the ideas are being developed, I feel it is still necessary to be open to gaining new sources of inspiration to allow ideas to evolve even further. It is also really important to research what market you are aiming for, as this can really effect the first stages of development. For me, research is a really exciting process, as it opens up endless possibilities.

What advice would you give to anyone interested in a career in fashion/ fashion forecasting?

Be very aware of what is happening around you, make the most of opportunities that come your way, be prepared to put in many hours and – most importantly – enjoy what you are doing!

Wendy Dagworthy

Wendy Dagworthy formed her own company in 1972 and two years later joined the prestigious London Designer Collections, where she subsequently became director from 1982–1990. She had huge success during the 1970s and 80s selling her collections to an international market and exhibited seasonally at London, Milan, New York and Paris, which confirmed the importance of her contribution to the international fashion industry. In 1989, she became course director at Central Saint Martins College of Art and Design, London.

She joined the Royal College of Art in 1998 where she became a professor and head of fashion, becoming head of the School of Fashion and Textiles in 2000. Her dedication and passion for the fashion industry is reflected in the overwhelming amount of work she undertakes for all aspects of the industry. She has been a judge of many art and design projects, awards and competitions and has given lectures all over the world. She has been a member of key international and professional committees and remains an external examiner for several major European colleges.

She was honoured in the 2011 New Year's Honours List and received an OBE for services to the fashion industry.

What is research?

The philosophy of the Royal College of Art's fashion courses is to nurture individual talent to produce innovative designers who will challenge and influence international fashion.

Research, innovation, creativity, versatility and individuality are the foundations of our philosophy.

The principle of personal research is the driving force behind the design process, encouraging students to pursue individual ideals with a fearless approach to investigating and questioning the boundaries of fashion.

'The principle of personal research is the driving force behind the design process... pursue individual ideals with a fearless approach to investigating and questioning the boundaries of fashion.'

Research – what and why?

Alexander Lamb

Alexander Lamb graduated from Manchester School of Art in 2009 with a first class honours degree in fashion and technology. He is currently studying his Masters in Menswear at The Royal College of Art in London. While at the RCA, he won the Umbro Design Award, was a finalist in the competition to design the costumes for the victory ceremonies at the London 2012 Olympic Games and most recently won The Brioni Tailoring award in 2011.

From his technical background, Alexander describes his design signature as function having a form, and giving his garments a unique and contemporary twist through the use of statement silhouettes.

What are your main sources of inspiration as a designer?

As a designer… I am interested in hidden collections/archives as a starting point for design. I like to reference forgotten items of clothing and details; not just the past, but artefacts from people's personal collections that are often overlooked. This can mean researching into old generic garments and the military, being informed by the delicate detailing and beautiful craftsmanship. Rather than replicating designs from the past, I like to work with certain elements, celebrating the forgotten details and construction methods; reviving them to create conversational yet contemporary menswear.

Do you have a signature style?

I often design with very masculine inspiration and silhouettes in mind but my handwriting in design develops very fluid yet sculpted forms. I aim to introduce interesting silhouettes to menswear and with these ingredients married together, create a contemporary look whilst producing truly wearable pieces.

Interview: Alice Palmer > Interview: Wendy Dagworthy > Interview: Alexander Lamb

Alexander Lamb

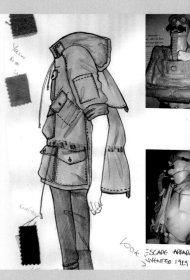

How do you start the design process from your research?

My background in design is technical, so a direction towards construction and functionality is a key element in the design process. I like to give 'function a form'.

Another main element in the design process is people's personal stories; this can often have an affect on colour/mood and silhouette, depending on the character or tribe. I like to use their stories to portray a personality or character through my clothing.

○ A/W11 printed parka.
○ Spec drawings and technical illustrations showing colour and fabric design development.
○ Toiling and silhouette development.
○ Alexander Lamb for Brioni design development.
○○ Illustration from Alexander Lamb A/W11.

Do you ever design a collection with one person in mind?

As a designer, I want to clearly understand who I am designing for and what my customers would desire from my work. I want to be able to work both creatively and critically in a time of change, as the current climate possibly represents a time when designers need to be concerned with much more than image alone.

Research – what and why?

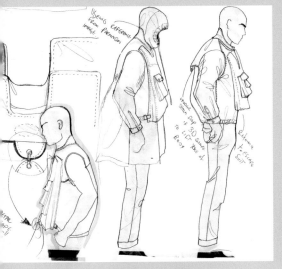

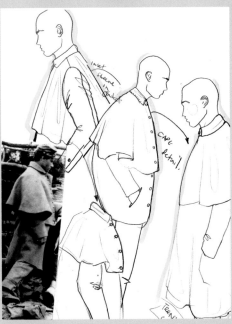

Interview: Wendy Dagworthy > Interview: Alexander Lamb > Interview: Daniel Pollitt

Daniel Pollitt

Daniel Pollitt graduated from Manchester Metropolitan University, UK with a BA Fashion Design degree in 2009. After an internship with Roland Mouret, he went on to work as an assistant designer for an outwear company based in London.

In 2010, Daniel went on to study a Masters Degree in Womenswear at the Royal College of Art, London.

Daniel states that his designs are strongly driven by an obsession with the female form, and he enjoys constructing clothes that bring out a woman's darker side.

How do you start the research process?

I like to approach my research with an open mind. I often begin by compiling imagery and mix this with information that intrigues me. Other times, I begin with sketching which develops into my initial design ideas. It all depends on what happens and how it naturally develops. One of the most exciting parts of design is the beginning, when you do not really know what is going to happen.

What kind of brief/constraints/direction/market do you work to?

At the beginning of a project, I find it best to collect as much information as possible before I start refining. Thinking about my customers can also influence the direction of my design; having this clear in my head helps me to create a vision or a certain look I am trying to achieve.

Do you set themes? If so, how and where do these start?

When gathering my research, I always try to use varied sources and themes, almost like ideas that clash with each other. Even if I do not end up using everything I have referenced, it helps me to produce a stronger concept. I normally begin with selecting three to four themes and explore their values separately. Once I feel this is complete, I piece them together – which is normally around the time that I begin my sketchbook and initial design work.

What are your sources of inspiration?

My inspirations come from various sources and all sorts of places. Sometimes it can be something as simple as a line, tone, shape, texture or colour. I am interested in architecture, sportswear, historical costume and 90s grunge.

Research – what and why?

○ Slash jersey textile
technique on neckline of dress.
◑ Final illustration of
womenswear dress design.

'One of the most exciting
parts of design is the
beginning, when you
do not really know what
is going to happen.'

Interview: Alexander Lamb > Interview: Daniel Pollitt

Daniel Pollitt

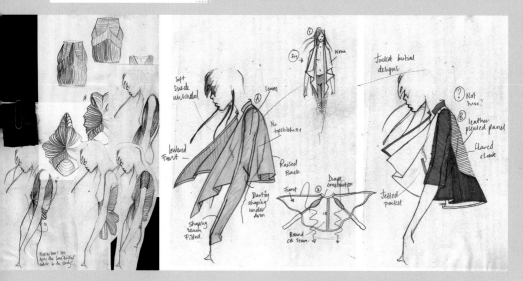

◑ Early sketchbook design analysis.

◐ Collaged design illustration.

How important is the research to the design process?

Research is crucial to the design process. One of the most exciting parts of designing is in the beginning when you don't really know what is going to happen. Without research, my design work would not materialize, as there would be nothing to underpin what I am trying to achieve.

Do you have sources that you repeat or revisit in seasons or collections?

Each collection and brief is not always entirely new; I like to revisit research and techniques from previous projects that did not work at that time. Sometimes, a sample I previously discarded becomes the basis on which I build my next collection. I try to keep as much of my design work as possible for future reference.

What advice would you give to anyone interested in a career in fashion/ fashion forecasting?

Fashion can be exhausting at times, as things do not always go to plan. Therefore, you must be self-driven and open-minded. Be brave and believe in yourself.

Research – what and why?

Fashion is not <small>something that</small> <small>exists in</small> dresses only. <small>Fashion is in the</small> sky <small>in the</small> street <small>fashion</small> <small>has to do with</small> ideas <small>the way we</small> live <small>what is</small> happening.

Coco Chanel

2

Now that you have a good understanding of what research is and what it needs to contain in order to be useful and relevant, you need to find out where to obtain this information.

In this chapter, we will explain how you go about choosing a concept and setting a theme – and whether that is narrative, conceptual or abstract. We also explain the differences between primary and secondary sources, as using both in your research will be essential. We will also explore the different sources of inspiration available, from museums and art galleries to the natural world and architecture.

When it comes to choosing a theme for your collection, you need to firstly consider how it responds to the brief (if there is one) and secondly, ensure that it will stimulate you to be creative. Words and images may well have already been explored in the brainstorming process (pages 32–33) and will therefore assist in the collation of ideas into a possible theme or concept.

A theme or concept is the essence of a good collection and is what makes it unique and personal to you. Remember: a good designer will explore aspects of their own personality, interests and viewpoints about the world around them, fusing them into a vibrant, innovative and credible collection. A theme may be driven by several different approaches, as explored in the following pages.

Abstract

This is where you work perhaps with an unrelated word or description, for example, 'surrealism'.

This word is then translated into a series of ideas or leads the approach to the research and design explored.

What images and words would you associate with surrealism? How might a garment eventually express this word?

Conceptual

This is where you might explore a variety of unrelated visual sources that can be drawn together because of similar or juxtaposed qualities. For example, a photograph taken of a piece of mineral rock and a shell, alongside a piece of pleated fabric and images of the artists Christo and Jeanne-Claude's installation work, such as of their wrapping of the Reichstag Building in Berlin, Germany with fabric.

This combination of information might also possess similar qualities that could be explored, translating into shapes, textures and colours in the design of your collection.

> 'It's great to tell a story in a collection, but you must never forget that, despite all the fantasy, the thing is about clothes.'
> John Galliano,
> Galliano, Colin McDowell,
> Weidenfeld & Nicolson

Narrative

Narrative, by its definition, means a written account of something, perhaps a story or a tale.

The designer John Galliano is famous for creating wonderful stories and characters for his collections, often creating a muse as his central focus; for example, the 1920's dancer Josephine Baker was inspiration in one collection, as was the Countess de Castiglione in another. Each of these characters brings style and also a personality to bear on the process; it also helps to direct the sources of research and design, as well as the final presentation of the collection.

It is important to remember that regardless of how you start the generation of ideas, it is the clothes that you will ultimately be judged on by the world's fashion buyers and press.

◑ Research board inspired by the work of Christo and Jeanne-Claude and pleating.

◑◑ Research board inspired by the work of surrealist artists Salvador Dali and Hans Bellmer.

Choosing a theme > What are primary sources?

Primary sources are the findings that you have collected or recorded first hand. In other words, they are the objects that you have drawn directly from, for example, anatomical references from a museum of natural history.

Primary sources are generally recorded through drawings or photographs, and often provide greater sensory associations than just the object itself. For example, touch and smell may all recall memories and be included in the final design process.

○ Some examples of drawing in student sketchbooks, which have been largely inspired by natural history.

Secondary sources are the findings of other people. These may be found in books, on the Internet, or in journals and magazines, for example. They are just as important as primary sources of research and often allow you to see and read about things that are no longer around or that are not easily accessible.

It is vital that you understand both types of sources and that in any good research there is a balance of both. Primary sources will call upon your drawing talents and secondary sources will utilize your investigative skills – so be prepared to bring both together in your design research.

○ Further examples of student sketchbooks, drawing on both cultural and historical sources of inspiration.

You should now understand what research is and the elements it should contain in order for you to design from it. We have also explored the need for a concept or theme (see pages 46–47).

So where do you find the information you need in order to begin the process of gathering your research? Where do you go for sources of inspiration?

⊙ ⊙ **Student sketchbooks demonstrating inspirational material in the early research stages.**

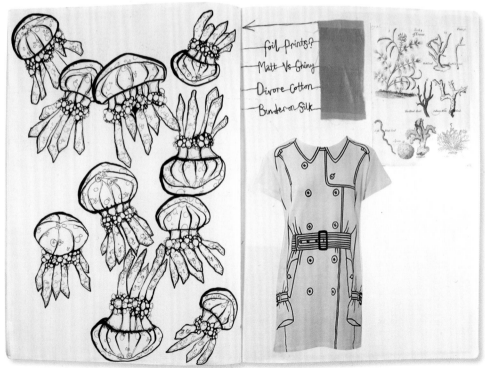

Ribbing

Online fashion resources

The Internet is probably the easiest place to start, as it is the most accessible way of gathering information, images and text from all over the world. Using search engines to find websites that may be dedicated to the subject you have begun to look at is often the fastest way to find inspiration.

Remember: research is not just about visual inspiration, it is also about tangible, practical things, such as fabric sourcing. The Internet allows you to get in touch with companies and manufacturers who may be able to provide you with fabric samples, trimmings and specialist skills in production or finishing.

Take a look at specialist online fashion-related resources, such as costume archives, manufacturing and fabric wholesalers, specific trend and forecasting companies, and industry events such as Premier Vision, which showcases the latest fabrics from around the world. Having a good 'fashion awareness' is essential if you are to progress within the industry.

Fashion blogs

Blogs are a huge growth area in the fashion media industry. Within the global community that we all now live in, fashion blogs enable people to review, discuss and follow styles and trends from all around the world. In terms of research value, blogs offer an opportunity to gather style and trend information very easily and apply this to market awareness and new product development.

Fashion blogs can be categorized into many different fields, such as street style, high-street fashion, haute couture, shoes, handbags, eco-fashion and celebrity style, for instance.

Fashion blogs are increasingly becoming a vital part of the mainstream fashion media and are easily accessible by a huge and diverse market. Blogs are also now integral to the PR strategies of many large fashion companies, as they provide an opportunity for them to promote their products and simultaneously enable interactive communication with their customers.

Blogs can be written by anyone, but in general they fall into three distinct categories, in terms of whether they are written by insiders, outsiders or aspiring insiders.

Insiders are those who work in the fashion industry and are able to offer professional opinions and points of view on current trends or products.

> 'These days, to have one finger on the fashion pulse, you need to have the other on the computer mouse, reading or writing the latest blogs.'
> Karen Kay
> *Daily Mail* (2007)

Outsiders are those people who don't work within the fashion industry but have a strong opinion on fashion due to their personal interest in it as a consumer.

Finally, aspiring insiders are those people who wish to work in the industry and see blogging as a new media and a means of gaining attention and possible employment. Many of these aspiring insiders have indeed found employment and are often invited to feature on mainstream media websites and to comment on events such as fashion weeks and individual designer shows.

Fashion and trendspotting blogs

www.coolhunting.com
This website has a global team of editors and contributors who sift through innovations in design, technology, art and culture to create their award-winning publication, consisting of daily updates and weekly mini-documentaries.

www.costumegallery.com
Costume Gallery is an extensive site of 40,000 pages and 85,000 images aimed at students, designers and those involved in textile manufacture and research.

www.fashion.net
This is a searchable site providing a good starting point with sections on beauty, designers and magazines, as well as shopping links to other sites.

www.fashioncapital.co.uk
Fashion Capital offers up-to-the-minute fashion industry news and other items of interest to fashion professionals.

www.papermode.trendland.net
Paper Mode is a fashion editorial dream! It showcases the latest (and older) editorials from every fashion magazine imaginable, and is constantly updating and enlarging this incredible archival resource.

www.showstudio.com
SHOWstudio.com is an award-winning fashion website, founded by fashion photographer Nick Knight. It works with the world's most sought-after filmmakers, writers and cultural figures to create visionary online content, exploring every facet of fashion through moving image, illustration, photography and the written word.

www.stylebubble.co.uk
Susie Bubble's blog and website has become synonymous within the fashion industry as one of the first fashion blogs to be picked up by mainstream fashion press and design houses. Her blogs from the front row provide quick and immediate access to the key shows of the season, as well as showcasing emerging talent.

www.thecoolhunter.co.uk
The Cool Hunter celebrates creativity in all its modern manifestations. The Cool Hunter is a leading authority on all things creative and a global hub for what's cool, thoughtful, innovative and original.

www.thesartorialist.blogspot.com
The sartorialist blogspot has images of people on the streets of New York and Paris. The main focus is on the clothes that they wear and the shops that they inhabit. The street style imagery is supported by sharp and brief commentaries.

www.wgsn.com
WGSN is Worth Global Style Network, which provides online news, trends and an information service for the fashion and style industries.

d having an
n essential part
nd magazines
are a good place to develop this knowledge.

Magazines are a great source of information and potential inspiration for the designer; they can firstly provide you with images of the latest trends, styles and garments from other designers in the industry, and secondly give you insight into other aspects you should consider as a designer, for example, lifestyle and cultural interests that may affect the market you wish to design for.

Knowing your subject is vital to the success of any design project or brief. Fashion by its very definition is about current styles and trends, so online magazines are more able to quickly update and refresh new and changing information about current styles and ideas.

Online magazines

Online magazines also allow for mixed media presentations of information, so in addition to written content there is the ability to show visuals not only through photographs but also video and film footage, such as the latest catwalk shows or designer interviews.

As the cost of setting up an online magazine is relatively low, there are far more diverse and niche market sites set up to cater for specific consumers and markets of fashion. Such areas of interest, for instance, may feature the latest collections and up-to-the-minute fashion news, lifestyle, trends, retail information, industry and manufacturing, global street life and youth subculture genres.

Online magazines allow you to review and research the most current information as well as access new and up-and-coming creatives, designers, stylists, photographers and writers from around the world.

Access to this wealth of information and insight into the industry is vital to any well-informed designer and should play a major part of any design student's good practice when it comes to researching a new product or idea.

○○○ **A small selection of inspirational books.**

Online magazines

www.fashion156.com
Presents fashion and style in a realistic, authentic and approachable manner, showcasing the work of more avant-garde designers, the freshest graduates and the most desirable pieces from the best collections.

www.fashionista.com
Features the personalities, companies, events and trends that shape the fashion universe.

www.iht.com
Suzy Menkes' fashion pages from the International Herald Tribune.

www.style.com
Style.com is a very comprehensive fashion magazine produced by CondeNet. It hosts an excellent coverage of collections which can be searched by season, designer and trend.

www.vogue.co.uk
Vogue Online is the web version of the UK monthly. Contains daily news, interviews and job opportunities.

www.wwd.com
Womenswear daily is the free online version of the American fashion retailers' daily newspaper. Offers headlines, classified ads, links to other sites and subscription details, plus a preview of full online version.

Libraries, books and journals

A library is a wonderful place to begin your research as it can offer immediate references for images and text in the form of books and journals. A library allows you to explore aisles of books on subjects that you may not have initially considered during your brainstorming sessions. There is something special about leafing through a book; the smell, touch and visual stimulus they can provide are often forgotten when simply looking on the Internet. Books are things that are themselves crafted and designed. Viewing an original manuscript of Victorian drawings is far more inspirational than seeing them on a computer screen.

You should be able to access a library in almost every town and city and it can provide you with a general and broad selection of books. However, if you are studying at college or university, you should have access to a much more specific range of books and journals that will be more usefully related to your interests and the courses taught there.

What are secondary sources? > **Sources of inspiration** > Exercise 2: Recycled garment manipulation

Museums and art galleries

Museums are a wonderful source of primary research as they contain a huge and diverse array of objects, artefacts and historical treasures. There are often museums dedicated to specific interests, such as the military, science, natural history or the arts.

Places such as the Victoria and Albert museum in London or The Metropolitan Museum of Art in New York are vast palaces of global art, design, history and culture. They offer the designer a great starting point to the research process, enabling you to explore many galleries and rooms dedicated to different subjects, countries and periods. The possibilities are under one roof, but have the potential to be endless.

Art galleries are also an essential part of the research process as they offer inspiration for subject matter, colour, texture, print and surface embellishment.

Artists have directly influenced many collections by fashion designers. For example, Versace used Andy Warhol's Marilyn Monroe Pop Art print from the 1960s as the inspiration for a print on a dress, Yves Saint Laurent incorporated Mondrian's graphic work on to a shift dress during the 1960s and Elsa Schiaparelli worked with the surrealist artist Salvador Dali on many pieces during the 1930s.

⦾ Holly Fulton S/S10, inspired by the Scottish artist Eduardo Paolozzi's 'Calcium Light Night' painting of 1975–6.
Catwalking.com

Paintings can also provide you with a picture of life and dress from a period or country where photography was not present, for example, Renaissance art and sculpture in Rome or perhaps scriptures from Egyptian times. Most towns and cities have a central museum and art gallery, so it is wise to explore what is available as you may find hidden treasures worth further investigation.

Choosing what to research

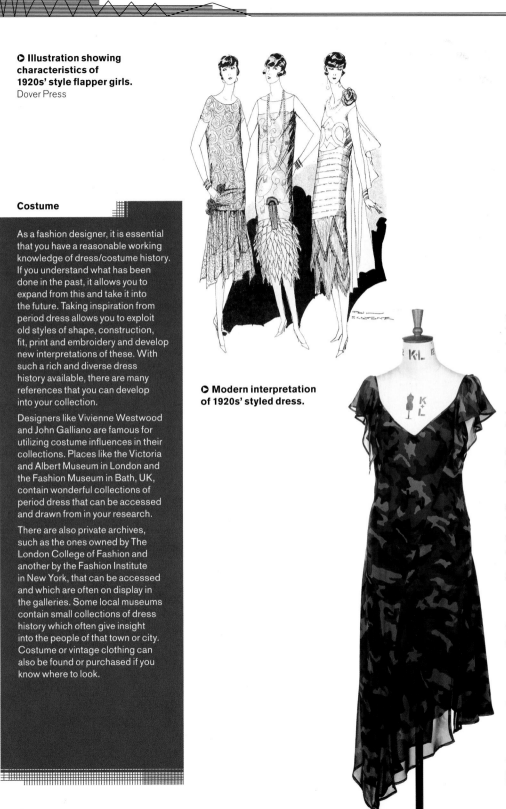

○ **Illustration showing characteristics of 1920s' style flapper girls.**
Dover Press

Costume

As a fashion designer, it is essential that you have a reasonable working knowledge of dress/costume history. If you understand what has been done in the past, it allows you to expand from this and take it into the future. Taking inspiration from period dress allows you to exploit old styles of shape, construction, fit, print and embroidery and develop new interpretations of these. With such a rich and diverse dress history available, there are many references that you can develop into your collection.

Designers like Vivienne Westwood and John Galliano are famous for utilizing costume influences in their collections. Places like the Victoria and Albert Museum in London and the Fashion Museum in Bath, UK, contain wonderful collections of period dress that can be accessed and drawn from in your research.

There are also private archives, such as the ones owned by The London College of Fashion and another by the Fashion Institute in New York, that can be accessed and which are often on display in the galleries. Some local museums contain small collections of dress history which often give insight into the people of that town or city. Costume or vintage clothing can also be found or purchased if you know where to look.

○ **Modern interpretation of 1920s' styled dress.**

Travel

As a designer, it is important to explore
and discover your environment and realize
that everything around you has the potential
to be research. Therefore, the ability to
travel must also be an important part of the
research process. Looking at and learning
from other cultures and countries can provide
you with a wealth of information that can be
translated into contemporary fashion design.

Large design companies will often send
their design team abroad to research
for their collections, with a view to them
gathering old treasures, pieces of fabric,
artefacts, garments, jewellery and
accessories – anything they think could
be used as inspiration. Photographs
and drawings are a vital part of recording your
experiences of travelling to another country.
As an aspiring designer, it is important to
consider that a holiday abroad can also be
an opportunity to gather research.

> 'The novelties of one
> generation are only
> the resuscitated fashions
> of the generation
> before last.'
> George Bernard Shaw

Flea markets and second-hand shops

We have already discussed that research is about poking and prying, sourcing information and always being on the look out for references for design. Flea markets and second-hand shops offer you an ideal opportunity to discover old treasures, discarded artefacts and vintage or period clothes by simply wandering in and around them.

Most of the great fashion capitals of the world have good areas to search for such markets and shops; for example, Portobello Road Market in London, Greenwich Village in New York and Montmartre in Paris.

Some designers have built their individual design identity on using vintage or recycled components in their collections.

O **Inspiration board** showing examples of world costume and dress.

O **The famous Portobello Market in London is a treasure trove of vintage and antique finds.**

What are secondary sources? > **Sources of inspiration** > Exercise 2: Recycled garment manipulation

Recycled garment manipulation

With flea markets, second-hand shops and vintage stores providing such a wealth of material and inspiration, it is important to consider how this tangible inspiration can be used for potential design direction. Not only is it simply about looking at and learning from the objects and garments found; it can also be about how they can be manipulated, draped and deconstructed to discover new and hidden directions. Furthermore, the use of recycling is not only an inventive way of researching and developing design ideas, but is also one that has a sustainable and ethical consideration.

Working with recycled garments through draping, disassembling them and deconstructing them can provide you with many new and inventive ideas, and is a great way to start analyzing and interpreting your research. By taking garments apart, you can also start to learn about how they were constructed and even begin to understand basic flat pattern development.

Deconstruction of recycled garments is a great way to begin to push against the traditional constraints of fashion. Exploring proportion and scale, placement and displacement, symmetry and asymmetry, as well as the juxtaposition of fabrics, textures, prints and garment types is a great way to get you thinking and developing early ideas for garments and design possibilities.

What happens when you take a traditional men's trenchcoat and take apart the different components, such as the collar, sleeves, stormflaps and belt, and blend and drape them onto a ladies' jersey dress, or even a classic men's shirt? The hybrid garment becomes new and exciting and offers up avenues for further exploration and design. It is important that you record all of your experimentation either through photography or drawing, as these three-dimensional experiments will provide you with further research and analysis to work from in the design process later on.

○ **Vintage-inspired ideas in student sketchbook.**

Recycled garment manipulation

In this exercise, you will explore and record three-dimensional recycled garment manipulation and deconstruction techniques. You will need to source a range of second-hand garments from a charity shop or flea market. It is best if you can gather several different types of garments in different fabrics and perhaps even look for non-garment items to drape, such as tablecloths and shawls.

You will need access to a mannequin or dress stand, either full-scale or half-scale, as well as pins, scissors, quick-stitch unpick, a camera and drawing media. Look at each of the items you have found. Place them in their usual form on the dress stand. Make a drawing and/or take a photograph. Analyze and record the different components that make up the garment, such as seams, panels, collars, cuffs and sleeves, and details such as pockets, belts, epaulettes, buttons, lapels, stormflaps, pleats and linings.

Now that you have fully explored and examined the garment as it is, it is time to model and drape with the garment from different viewpoints. So, firstly turn the garment upside down. If it has sleeves or legs, what happens when these are used for a different purpose or are connected? Can a collar become a hemline detail? Can you turn a sleeve inside out to form a pocket? Reposition the centre front to the centre back, or even create a side-seam opening perhaps.

Suggested items could be some from the following list:

- men's large cotton shirts
- T-shirts or jersey items
- a man's (or a woman's) suit jacket and trousers
- trenchcoat
- ladies' printed dresses
- denim jackets and jeans
- old leather coat
- lace trims or table cloths
- accessories such as belts, large or decorative bags, shawls, stoles and furs (depending on your views).

Now take another garment from your stock and quickly unpick it or simply cut it open at the seams. Disassemble the components, such as the sleeves, collars, cuffs, waistbands, pockets and linings. Now start to pin and model these onto the other garment; consider both regular and irregular placement. Work with different combinations of garments, such as a dress and a coat, or a shirt and trousers. How do the different pieces start to work against and with one another?

As you explore a range of combinations, make sure that you record each of them using either your camera or through drawing. Record the garments from all sides, as details and silhouettes could be created on all 360 degrees of the stand.

Architecture

Fashion and architecture have a great deal in common, it may surprise you to learn! They actually start from the same point – the human body. They both protect and shelter, while also providing a means to express identity, whether it is personal, political, religious or cultural.

Fashion and architecture also express ideas of space, volume and movement and have parallel practices in the way that they exploit materials from flat two-dimensional surfaces to complex three-dimensional forms. It is because of this common factor that architecture is a wonderful subject matter to explore for research as a fashion designer.

Like costume, architecture can express period trends and has often linked itself with social interests, as well as changes in technology, in particular the use of new materials and production techniques.

You only need to look at the work of the Spanish architect Gaudi in the late 1800s and early 1900s and his interest in the natural world, and the related art and dress movement his work was part of, to see how closely fashion and architecture are linked.

More recently, Japanese designers such as Yohji Yamamoto and Comme des Garçons have demonstrated clear similarities in the garments that they create and the contemporary architecture that they are surrounded by.

◐ Linear and structural qualities can be seen in the cables of New York's Brooklyn Bridge.

◑◐ Clear visual and structural links can be made between this Balmain dress (A/W 09) and the Lyon-Satolas Airport Railway station, designed by Santiago Calatrava in 1994.

'Fashion is architecture. It is a matter of proportions.'
Coco Chanel

The natural world

The natural world provides a vast and diverse source of inspiration for gathering primary information. It is a source of visual stimuli that can inspire all of the key elements you need to determine in your research, such as shapes, structures, colours, patterns and textures.

Your interest may lead you to look at rare birds of paradise or butterflies and insects. It may be that you explore the patterns of snakes or the jungle foliage of a rainforest. The opportunities are endless – and as a source of inspiration, the natural world is one that is consistently explored by designers.

◐◑ **Catwalk fashion which draws inspiration from nature, as in this floral-inspired blouse and skirt by Erdem (S/S11) (above), and Dior haute couture dress (S/S11) reminiscent of the beautiful colours and petal shapes of tulips (right).** Catwalking.com

◐◑ **Illustration and books referencing the natural world.** Illustration courtesy of Dover Press

FLORA
By Nick Knight

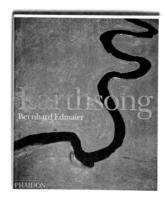

Earthsong
Bernhard Edmaier
PHAIDON

Film, theatre and music

The film, theatre and music industries have always had very close links to fashion. The famous Hollywood starlets of the 1930s and '40s were always photographed dressed in garments by French designers such as Lanvin, Balenciaga and Dior. The glamorous, unattainable lives they led only added to the allure of the clothes that they wore, spurring designers on to create even more fantastic pieces.

In more recent times, it has been rock and pop stars who have tended to excite and create a lifestyle that people want to aspire to. Through associations with designers and brands, they often promote collections in videos, promos, movies and publications. Vivienne Westwood and Malcolm MacLaren, for instance, famously dressed the Sex Pistols in the 1970s and started a whole new subcultural movement called punk.

The links between music and fashion are today so close that we are now in an era when the big American hip hop and rap stars, such as Sean John, Jay Z and Kanye West, routinely create their own fashion labels and promote them through music.

Meanwhile, former popstar Victoria Beckham has readily made the transition from fashion muse to fashion designer, having shown a credible line at New York Fashion Week for several seasons running and to significant critical acclaim.

Due to such close associations between the music and film industries, these are certainly areas that you may wish to explore as sources of inspiration; whether it be to start your collection with a muse, or by looking to a movie theme as a possible direction to research more fully.

◑ Charlie Chaplin inspired Galliano menswear S/S11.
Catwalking.com

◐◑ Student sketchbooks demonstrating the influence of various music icons (Jimi Hendrix, Adam Ant and Eric Clapton) as sources of inspiration.

Choosing what to research

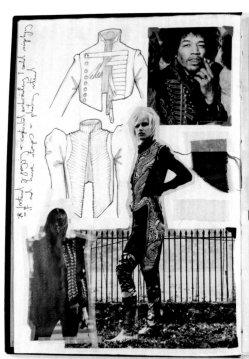

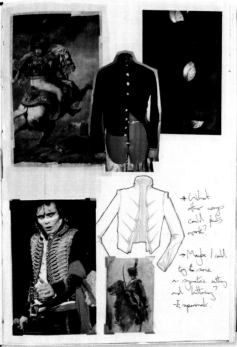

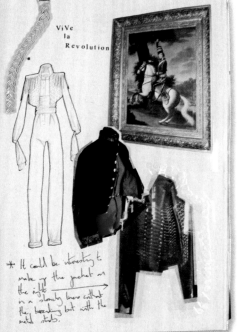

Street and youth culture

We have already looked at the importance of contemporary trends and how these are often related to global and cultural interests and changes in taste. And we have referred to the 'bubble-up effect' – how trends can form on the street and influence catwalk designs and ultimately what is fashionable in the mainstream.

It is therefore essential that the research process should include possible inspiration from the street and from subcultures or special interest groups. Influences may come from trends in clothing styles, for example the Harujuku kids from Tokyo, the skateboarders from Downtown LA or the club kids from the 1990s in New York.

All of these subculture youth groups have an identity and style of their own and have influenced many designers' collections in the past, from the clothes to the make-up and styling. By looking to and experiencing the street and what it has to offer at any one moment, in any one city, you can filter out trends and interests and identify what is fresh, new and directional. But street culture can also be an area to look back on as old street styles have also influenced contemporary designers.

◯◯ Here are some images of original punk subculture of the late 1970s/early 1980s.
© Richard Braine/PYMCA (top)
© Judith Erwes/PYMCA
(second from bottom)
© Mr Hartnett/PYMCA
(second from top, and bottom)

◯ From the punk-inspired Balmain S/S11 collection.
Catwalking.com

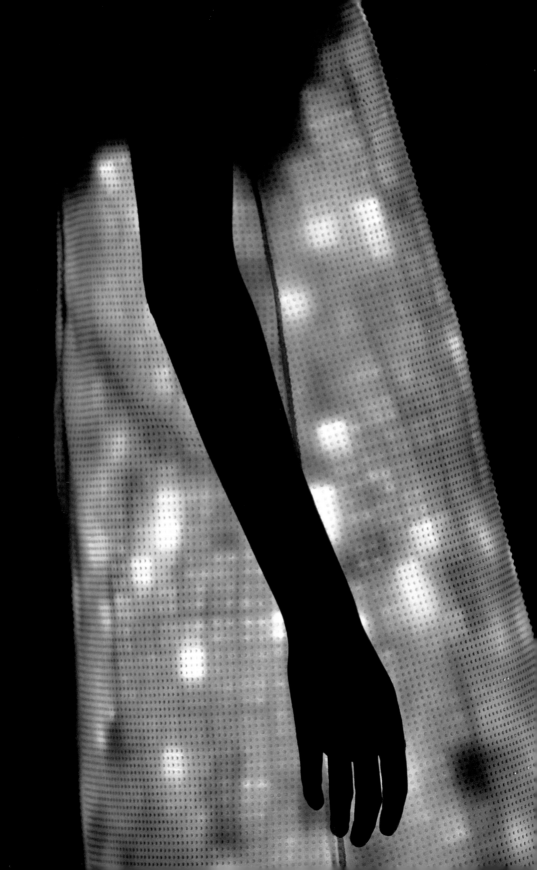

New technologies

The development of new technologies in the fashion industry is an element that has always played a role in the design and research process.

During the 1960s, there was a huge technological breakthrough in synthetic fibres and an interest in space and the future that inspired a generation of young designers, such as Mary Quant, André Courrèges and Pierre Cardin.

More recently, there have been significant technological developments in digital printing. Designers such as Basso & Brooke and Manish Arora have made full use of these new techniques in their signature prints for their collections. There are also designers such as Issey Miyake, Hussein Chalayan and Junya Watanabe that construct their garments out of a whole new generation of smart fabrics and materials.

E-textiles (or 'smart textiles'), for instance, enable computing and digital components to become embedded into everyday garments as 'wearable technology'.

As a designer, it is important to consider such new technologies – as well as future ones – when you are beginning a new collection.

Forecasting and trend agencies

Forecasting and trend agencies can also be a possible source of inspiration.

As already discussed, having an awareness of street cultures, new trends, new technologies and global interests is important when it comes to researching for a new collection or the development of a new brand.

Tracking trends is not just about looking at fashion, but also about looking at demographics, behaviour, technologies and lifestyle. Consumer analysis will often help a designer create the right clothes and accessories for people in the future.

Companies will spend huge amounts of their budgets to gain this sort of insight into the market and what they then need to focus their ideas towards.

Fashion forecasting agencies are companies set up to support the industry and specifically look at current trends and cultural pursuits. They are, through market research, able to offer the designer a glimpse into ideas and directions that are becoming popular in society. These ideas can take the form of colours, fabrics, details and shapes, all of which are essential to the creative process as a fashion designer.

The information these agencies produce can be accessed through specialist magazines and trend books, as well as through presentations at trade fairs such as Premier Vision in Paris.

Read the full interview with the trend forecasting agency WGSN on pages 146–147.

○ **Hussein Chalayan A/W07 Airborne collection featuring LED-illuminated garments.**
Catwalking.com

Exercise 2: Recycled garment manipulation > **Sources of inspiration** > Interview: Dr Noki

Sustainability and ethics

Fashion makes an important contribution to society. It creates jobs and products that satisfy fundamental human needs. Yet it can also damage individuals and societies more widely through poor working practices, and the detrimental psychological and ecological effects of consumerist fashion. A fashion piece cannot in itself create sustainability – this is created by the way in which we design, make, wear, discard and reincarnate it. We need to design in a way that means we engage in fashion in a way that is sustainable.

◑◐◒ Ada Zanditon creates high-end, desirable ready-to-wear that is sculptural, innovative and features Ada's unique illustrations and prints. Ethical manufacturing and sustainable fabric choices are a core part of the brand philosophy.
Ada Zanditon AW10, © Paul Persky (below); Ada Zanditon AW11, © Sarah Brimley (right)

In a society obsessed with instant gratification and conspicuous consumption or 'fast fashion', it's easy to dismiss fashion design as frivolous. Skirt lengths and denim washes appear inconsequential when juxtaposed with real-world concerns like climate change, economic strife, water shortages, hunger and malnutrition. But if you consider the fact that clothing is something we envelop our bodies with every single day, to ignore the apparel industry's environmental and social impact would be simply negligent.

Changing fashion practices to improve the well-being of workers, consumers, designers and producers is central to a more sustainable future. The impact of the fashion sector on natural resources and ecosystems is substantial. There is an urgent need to reduce the negative effects of producing and consuming fashion. The use of organic clothing, produced without toxic pesticides and dipped in low-impact dyes is just one of the ways in which we, as designers, can start to change the very real impact that fashion has on the global environment.

Sustainability is worth considering when designing. Not only will it make you more aware of current trends within this movement, but it will also give you the edge when leaving university and entering the industry. Try and be inspired to think about and act on what you can do to make a difference in fashion and textiles, and how you can contribute towards building a sustainable future.

Dr Noki

Dr Noki studied at Edinburgh School of Art. Before setting up his own label, he worked with Helen Storey, Whitaker Malem and Owen Gastor from whom he learnt 'eco-thinking, arts and crafts and futuristic thinking' respectively. Noki is a subversive artist/designer, customizer and stylist based in the East End of London, having been dragged up in the Old Street/Shoreditch areas circa 1995, who is famously anonymous, recognizable only by the 'SOB' (Suffocation Of Branding) masks that he wears.

Noki is an anagram and pun, a playful subversion on the IKONic globalized fashion brand. Noki experiments with customization by collaging the 'sustainable canvas' together with creative cutting, stitching, appliqué and silk-screen printing, thereby creating a new genre of street couture.

How did you get started with the whole idea of using rag or recycled garments as a way of designing?

The initial idea behind Noki was as a magazine idea called NOKI-POD back in 1996, where the pages were to be an artistic visual aid subverting the message of advertising by providing a beautiful picture, rather than the generic commercial visuals you got in the normal magazine format back then, with the branding message put as listings at the back in the small print. This never worked out, so I put the idea and energy I had created into subverting the branded message, shape and function of the not so humble T-shirt.

Do you have a political statement or ethical statement to make with your work?

There is definitely a political edge to Noki, but this is not so much directed towards the government; it is more about the power that the superbrands have over our consumerist ways through creating subliminal need through multimedia advertising. I achieved this awareness through working at MTV in Camden, London as a stylist for the presenters. It was not until I had read the book *Culture Jamming* by Kalle Lassen that I realized how much power the modern brand actually has over our lives through advertising. I just felt a need to create a contemporary statement that did not alienate myself as a lover of brand design and imagery, but to perhaps use the brands' leftover products and branding itself as an artistic Noki statement or 'one-off'.

○ **Dr. Noki A/W08.**
Catwalking.com

○ **A Dr. Noki customized dress.**
Photographer: Axel Hoedt

Do you always start the design process with recycled garments?

When I first started creating Noki customization, it was all about the brand print on the front and how cracked it was, followed by the state of the fabric. The more washed out the better, especially black as it reminded me of a dusty layering, as if 'the bomb' had gone off and the fall-out had settled on the garment. It was a kind of reflection on how my mind had shifted to be able to think these left-of-centre ideas, which are now seen as normal aesthetics associated with the 'customized' look. All the shapes I've evolved through Noki are created by studying the garments and seeing how I can cleverly manipulate them, like the super brands do to us!

Do you have a research process?

The only research I need to do is to know whether it has come from a second-hand/dead-stock source; the rest of the Noki process just flows from manipulating the product into a different way of looking at it. There is, however, a very strong leaning towards colour, then texture; if something does not feel right to the touch, a potential client will reject the piece again. So a sort of research has taken place by knowing what the client will accept.

Richard Sorger

Richard Sorger graduated from Middlesex Polytechnic in 1991 and worked in Milan before returning to work for a London-based designer. In 2006, Richard started designing his eponymous label. In 2009, he launched his second line, RJS by Richard Sorger, which he sells worldwide. He has been commissioned to produce special pieces for Swarovski Unbridled and for the Victoria and Albert Museum, who acquired one of his dresses for their permanent collection in 2009.

Recently, he has collaborated with Meadham Kirchhoff, Manolo Blahnik (for Meadham Kirchhoff) and ASOS. In 2006, he co-authored the book *The Fundamentals of Fashion Design* (AVA Publishing). He is currently a senior lecturer in Fashion at Middlesex University, London.

How important is research in your working practice?

I think research is fundamental to the design process. I have to design several collections each year and so I need to find new inspiration each time to keep my work fresh.

What is the most enjoyable part of the process?

The initial research stage is exciting because anything could happen design-wise. The initial design stage can be a bit traumatic before I get into my stride, but when the first samples turn up and we open the box... that's always a heart-in-mouth exciting moment.

How do you start the research process? Do you start by looking at what sold last season?

When you run your own label, you're constantly learning from the mistakes and successes of each season. To begin with I was very concerned at how expensive the pieces were working out at wholesale, but the buyers I've met generally didn't raise an eyebrow. It's always a good idea to have some pieces that have a low entry-level price as you're seeing buyers who have different markets, but I'm lucky that with some of the pieces I don't have to compromise the design because of the cost – my pieces look expensive. I'm a believer in 'evolution' not 'revolution'; I don't believe in changing everything each season.

◐◐ **Richard Sorger S/S09, bias-cut agate dress in nude.**

◐ **Richard Sorger S/S09, wood-grain dress.**

◐ **Richard Sorger S/S09, crab spider dress.**

Photographer (all images): Jez Tozer

Richard Sorger

What are your sources of inspiration?

Like most designers, I'm constantly on the look-out for new inspiration. I produce two collections a year and I often get private commissions and projects for a specific client, so you sometimes have to come up with an idea at the drop of a hat. I regularly visit galleries and museums and some of the things that inspire me can have an effect in an abstract rather than literal way, just a mood or a colour. I also like the thinking behind a lot of contemporary design – furniture and product design. But my main source of inspiration at the moment is natural history. I hate to admit it but I like zoos – the last time I went I got over-excited about the vultures and other raptors. But I haven't used them. Yet.

Do you set themes or a narrative to your collections?

I try to, but if a theme gets in the way of a good idea I'm not precious. A collection has to gel as a whole, but rather than doing this through the theme, it can be done through the colour and the techniques that I use.

How do you collate your research?

I collate imagery in a sketchbook along with drawings and designs. I also put images, fabric etc. on a wall in my studio – things that inspire me but don't necessarily have a relevance to the collection that I'm working on. And I try to have a clear out every six months. I clear the wall and start again.

How important is the research to the design process for you?

Research is the best bit! Research is the point of unlimited possibilities. I get excited about what I'm potentially going to do and hunting down the right book, the right photograph, the right angle of an animal to draw from, is a challenge I relish.

How do you start the design process from the research?

After the optimism of the research, there's the pessimism of the initial design work. It takes a while to 'hit' the designs that I know will work and that satisfy me. And it's a stage I go through each time I sit down to design a collection, so I always try to remind myself that it's only a phase and that I'll 'break through'. So far I've been right.

With a collection that uses a variety of images, I find it really helps me to draw the subject matter. It's a pleasure to draw and it's also when I learn how to draw, for example, the curve of a snake's head from different angles or the line of a piece of fairground 'flash' artwork. I can't just sit down with a garment pattern in front of me and convincingly draw a line without the initial sketchbook work. It's also a time when I can process in my mind the research that I've gathered and it buys me time to think about what I might do with the actual designs.

Choosing what to research

How do you develop your designs into a collection?

I make sure that colours, fabrics, imagery and techniques are repeated within the collection, but generally what holds my collections together is the fact that everything is embroidered.

How do you differentiate your two lines each season? What is the creative link between the two?

Richard Sorger is the line where I allow my imagination (and costs) to run riot. RJS by Richard Sorger is a more commercial line where I think much more about cost and customer. In principal, the theme for the Richard Sorger main line will feed into the theme for the next season's RJS line, but it doesn't always work like that as another idea might come along when I'm planning the line.

How much do the sales from each season dictate the creative development of a new collection?

I think most designers have to be led by their sales to some extent, it's a business after all! I will integrate certain aspects into the next season if something sold well the previous season. I see it as an organic growth of ideas. If a piece or a technique of embroidery has sold well, I will be shameless and include it in some form in the next season.

What advice would you give to anyone interested in a career in fashion?

Some formal training is useful. There are exceptions to the rule, successful designers who haven't trained at college, but these come along about once in every few generations and generally fashion designers benefit from having done a degree or Masters course. Do a BA degree, then a Masters degree and intern for as many designers as you possibly can.

Get as much work experience as you're (financially) able to do – a job offer can often come from making yourself indispensable within a design house and even if it doesn't, it's experience to put on your CV. Don't be in a rush to set up your own label – make contacts and learn from other people's mistakes first.

It can also help if you're a 'niche' designer – if you design tailoring, accessories, or knitwear; for example, a buyer will know to come to you, rather than to go to a designer who does a bit of everything and not much of anything. But this can also work to your disadvantage if a buyer isn't interested in your speciality.

And it really helps if you're sociable, energetic and organized.

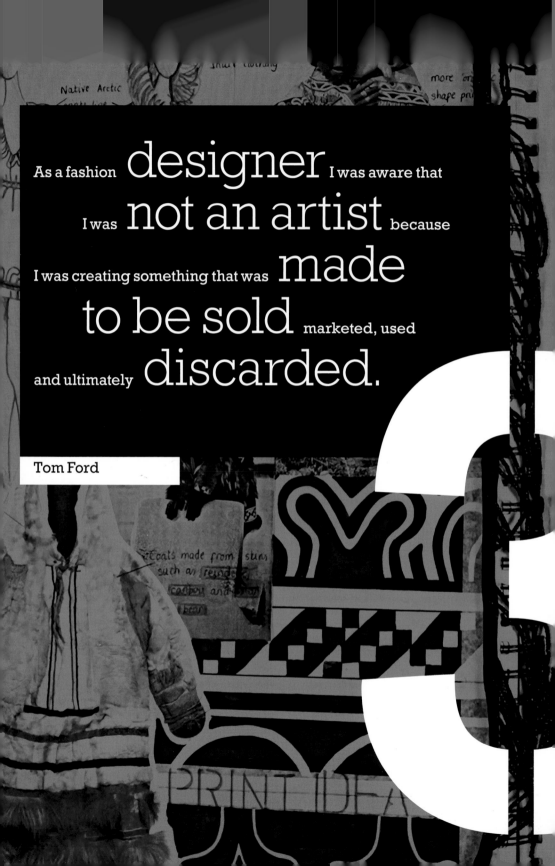

As a fashion **designer** I was aware that I was **not an artist** because I was creating something that was **made to be sold** marketed, used and ultimately **discarded.**

Tom Ford

on seal skin, 'Huma

lled birds on
onnt.

So far, you have discovered what research is and why you need it as a designer. You have also learnt where you can find it and the many sources of inspiration that are available to you.

In this chapter, we aim to explain how you piece together the information you have found. The format of a sketchbook is explained and different approaches to compiling your research, from drawing and collage to deconstruction and analysis, are examined.

The chapter uses different examples of sketchbook work to illustrate the many styles you can adopt. It also discusses how to move the research forward and begin to focus on key elements on mood- and concept-boards, in preparation for the design process.

Many Inuit when they see a
dog jump up from a sound
sleep and bark, believe
that the dog soon
some
the spir

LAZER
CUT....
These bird stencils could
be lazer cut of of garments
to create a print design.

As a designer, it is essential to explore and experiment with the idea of a sketchbook and how you compile your research.

A sketchbook is generally the place where you can collate and process all the information you have collected and it can become a very personal and individual space for ideas.

⟳ Cork pinboard used as storyboard for initial ideas.
⟳⟳ Example of drawing in a student sketchbook.

Assembling your research

Sketchbooks have traditionally been collated in book format with designers choosing the format and size that they take. A sketchbook can, however, also be gradually gathered and created into something that is later bound, having allowed the designer the opportunity to select and edit material as necessary.

Research can also be presented as a series of storyboards. This is often the approach in a design studio, where images, photographs, drawings, fabrics and trimmings are stuck to an inspiration wall or a series of moodboards.

The sketchbook can also be a tool to describe and illustrate a collection, and the journey you have taken, to others. This is often essential information, as it will show how you perceive the world around you, and demonstrate your ability to be a creative thinker. It can also be shared with others in a design studio to ensure that you are all working to a common set of themes.

Research books are not merely scrapbooks filled with tear sheets and photographs, but a place of learning, recording and processing information. A sketchbook should explore and experiment with a variety of ways in which the information can be presented.

Hard and soft
Masculine V.s feminine
Utility V.s Decoration

Sketchbooks

Sketchbooks can be purchased brand new in a wide variety of sizes, weights of paper, colours and bindings. They can also be something that you make for yourself, allowing you to work on different qualities of paper, edit and order the work, before binding it. A sketchbook can also be created in a second-hand format, by working in an old novel or textbook, perhaps using the text as a background to the theme of the research.

Drawing

Drawing is a fundamental process and skill that you must explore and perfect. It is an ideal way to record information on the spot; in other words, it is a good way to gather primary research.

By using a variety of different drawing media, for example, pencils, inks and paints, you are able to exploit the qualities and styles of line, texture, tone and colour that can be gained from your sources of inspiration and add depth to your research and design.

To draw the whole or part of an object or picture you have sourced helps you to understand the shapes and forms that are contained within it; this, in turn, enables you to translate these lines into a design, or to see them clearly when you are cutting a pattern. Brush marks and textures explored through drawing may also translate into fabric references in your designs.

Understanding and developing your visual language skills is something that you will continue to do throughout the creative research process, and drawing is just one part of that.

○ **Further examples of drawing in student sketchbooks.**

Familiarity with varied drawing materials will provide you, the designer, with a stronger ability to interpret and exploit your research and analysis of your inspiration.

Capturing and recording ideas using varied materials and techniques is an important part of the sketchbook process, and the use of broad and varied media will help to direct and advance the research process.

Using creative drawing techniques and exploring research and analysis with mixed media combinations can help you to convey a style and create an aesthetic within your own creative work, as well as enabling you to develop your own visual language.

There are many different drawing materials and ways in which to apply them and it will only be through trial and error that you discover the ones that work best for you. Listed here are some of the materials that you can use when capturing and recording ideas, and developing your drawings.

Drawing utensils

Graphite pencils

When you think of drawing, the first thing that comes to mind is the use of a pencil; its varied grades from hard to soft allow you to easily create monochrome tonal and linear representations of the subject matter as well as interpret these drawings into early design ideas. Graphite pencils can be used to create a variety of textures within a drawing; techniques to explore would be smudging and highlighting with an eraser or using cross-hatching techniques to add texture and indicate fabric or pattern.

Biro and fine liners

Sketching with a biro or fine-liner pen can produce a similar result to a hard graphite pencil, but will often require the designer to work in a more linear and graphic style. Sketching can be done using techniques such as continuous line, straight line only and single line representation of objects. The use of a pen can offer varied styles and approaches to drawing and can often enhance the clarity of a design sketch.

Coloured pencils

These provide the designer with a very quick and clean method of sketching and introducing colour. Working with coloured pencils allows you to add-in much more detail and texture to a drawing; and if you work with watercolour pencils, the addition of a brush and water will allow for blending and highlighting effects. The water will dissolve the colour and introduce light and a transparent effect to the drawing. The water also allows for blending and mixing of colour on the page and can create depth and tone to any observational or design drawing.

Pastels and Conte Pencils

Pastels are created using dry, ground pigment mixed with a binder to form a paste, which when hardened, forms crayons or sticks. Pastels will allow the designer to create soft chalk-like marks and a velvety finish. Applying colour with pastels is often helped by the use of your fingers and can be gradually built up with strong highlights and smoky tones. A Conte pencil is made up of chalk that is bound with gum and oil, and allows the user to create a more intense and thick line. They are a harder, more precise medium than a pastel but can be used successfully alongside pastels to create expressive drawings and illustrations.

Inks, nibs and brushes

Ink is a liquid media and has an intense pigment capacity; when it is used, it can create wonderful intense colour with fluid lines, as well as when mixed with water for a more soft and transparent look. Used with brushes, it can cover much more of a drawing and give colour and tone to a large space; with a nib, it can be treated the same as a pen, giving sharper and more precise marks. Inks are a great medium to explore, as used with wet and dry paper they also react differently; used in combination with pencils and Conte crayons or even bleach, inks can give real depth and contrast to the designer's sketchbook.

Watercolour paints

These are based on the techniques of using water to create transparency and soft fluid renderings in your drawings. Using watercolour paints allows you to apply colour in layers, building up tones and shades gradually to show texture, light and form. Using washes and allowing them to dry before applying further colour or dry media such as pencils or pastels is a great way to experiment with texture and fabric rendering.

Marker pens and brush-tip pens

Working with marker or brush-nib pens is the most modern way of hand-rendering a drawing. They are particularly used for the design process as they are quick, clean and graphic in their finish. Marker pens come in all different colours and shades, and a good design student should always have at least two nude- or flesh-tone markers in slightly different shades for design drawing.

The use of collage in your research is another approach to collating information from different sources, for example, photographs, magazine cuttings and printouts from the Internet.

The images you select need not necessarily have anything immediately in common. A good collage will explore a variety of elements that have their own strengths and qualities, but in combination present new directions as a whole. When you are working with images, do not be restricted by the shape you have, for example, a rectangle or square; cut out the shapes and collage them together in a creative way instead. Think of Monty Python's collaged titles and the work of pop artist Peter Blake, who created the album cover for The Beatles' *Sgt. Pepper's Lonely Hearts Club Band*, when putting the information together. Scale, placement and selection are skills that you will start to learn as you explore this technique in your sketchbook.

Collage

Collage is described as the artistic composition of sticking bits of paper and photographs to a surface; but the word originally derives from the French word for 'glueing'.

⊙⊙ Images from student sketchbooks exploring the use of collage technique.

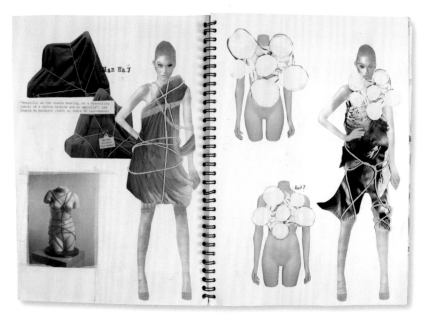

Collaged Designs

Juxtaposition

If collage is about cutting and sticking images together to create new ideas, then juxtaposition describes the process whereby you place images and fabrics side by side on the page.

Juxtaposition is a method that can often bring disparate elements together that share similarities; for example, the spiral shape of an ammonite fossil and a spiral staircase. Or the images may be suggestive of a fabric quality; for example, the textures of a starfish and coral may bring to mind an embossed or embellished fabric.

Juxtapose

This means to place or deal with things close together for contrasting effect. In terms of your research and design, this might relate to you placing images and fabrics side by side on your moodboard or in your sketchbook, for example.

◯ **Student sketchbook showing clear connections between the natural world and a range of textiles, demonstrating the use of juxtaposition.**

Deconstruction

To deconstruct or disassemble your research is to consider looking at the information from a new viewpoint or perspective. It may simply mean using a viewfinder and drawing an aspect of the object so that you focus on a detail to arrive at an abstract idea from the original source. But it may also mean breaking the information up like a jigsaw puzzle and reassembling it differently to create new lines, shapes and abstract forms to work from.

Disassemblage is also a process that relates to working with actual garments as a source of inspiration. It is a technique where you can take existing clothes apart and analyze how they have been created, perhaps taking patterns from them and looking at the construction details, which could then be translated into your own design ideas. This method of research has previously been discussed in more detail on pages 60–61.

◗ **This outfit clearly shows a deconstructed coat/dress by Comme des Garçons A/W11.**
Catwalking.com

Viewfinder

A viewfinder is a creative tool that allows you to conceal an object and then expose or view only a part of it. It can be made from a simple piece of card or paper and all you need to do is to cut a small square window into the centre of it. The window can be as small or as large as you wish, but the point is to offer you a view of only part of the object or image that you have sourced.

Your research may be initially quite abstract and varied, with many seemingly unrelated references sourced and explored. Methods like drawing, collage and juxtaposition are great for collating and experimenting with information, but cross-referencing your research is a technique that gets you to look for related visual references or ones that complement each other. These can then be grouped into early themes or concepts for you to explore further in the design process.

One example shown here demonstrates how a Naum Gabo sculpture and an Issey Miyake garment have similar qualities, for instance. All of these references come from different sources, but by bringing them together you can see how they relate to one another and form new directions for you to design from.

It is this mix of sources with similar qualities that is the essence of cross-referencing – and an essential part of any good research and the early analysis of it.

○○ Student sketchbooks demonstrating a variety of cross-referenced sources.

Unexpected

Hans Bellmer

Disfigurement

Distortion

Comme Des Garçons

Lumps and Bumps

Balenciaga tailoring

Puffball Sleeves

Bulbous Draped Skirts

White Spotted Jellyfish

As you begin to explore your research and compile ideas through collage and cross-referencing, you will start to see potential directions for your design. You will already have gathered information regarding shapes, textures, details, colour, print and perhaps historical references as part of your research. Now it's important that you begin to use your research and analyze it in terms of early design sketches.

○ **Mark Fast S/S 11 knitted dress exploring the ladder technique.** Catwalking.com

○ **Student sketchbook exploring early design from textures found in researched images.**

Why is analysis useful?

Early analysis requires you to draw shapes from the sources you have explored, and to experiment with mixed-media sketches, close-up and silhouette studies, linear drawings and details for construction.

These sketches should also explore ideas for texture, pattern and possible embellishments. The drawings need not necessarily be done on a figure and can simply be interpretations of the information that you have collected.

Colour should be something that is considered and explored through the use of mixed media, using the research as inspiration and extracting out possible ideas for colour palettes and combinations. The research should have contained some early ideas of texture and possible fabric manipulation and therefore these should form part of the early analysis for fabric design. You must begin to source and edit samples and trims that perhaps have similar qualities to the inspiration and show how your research has informed your thought processes into textural fabric ideas.

Another key stage of analysis is to try and translate early shapes from your research into quarter-scale pattern experiments or modelling on a stand (see pages 112–115). This is a three-dimensional approach to analysis, and by experimenting with and translating the information gathered, you will begin to see the potential for garment ideas and record this through photography and sketching. This is an extremely valuable part of the research and design process and is one that is explored more fully in chapter 4.

Through the early stages of research, compilation and analysis, you will start to have a much clearer direction and focus for your design concept. Each of these stages will have given you important inspiration and information to work with as a designer. The analysis will have drawn out some of the key elements that you must consider when designing a collection, such as shape, colour, fabric, details, print and embellishment.

This next stage is simply about focusing your mind using your sketchbook and creating a series of pages that clearly identify the elements that you wish to work from.

This focus also allows other people to interact with your vision; in other words, if you were working as a team, this is the point at which other members of the team could respond to the direction that the research was taking and add their input or suggestions for the collection.

This focusing of the key elements can also be presented as a series of moodboards, storyboards or concept-boards.

○ Student sketchbook illustrating key influences, inspiration, fabric and colour palette development.

Focus research pages

In this exercise, you need to highlight some of the key aspects of your research and compile a set of concept or focus pages.

Firstly, remember what you have explored and researched from the various sources of inspiration. Then try to select and edit the best elements that could be developed further or that relate to early design opportunities.

Now try to compile something that relates to each of the categories discussed previously (and listed again, below) in order that your research and design starts from a broad set of ideas and topics:

- shapes and structures
- details
- colour
- textures
- print and embellishment
- historical influences
- cultural influences
- contemporary trends.

The point of gathering, grouping and focusing the research into a set of pages or storyboards is so that you can review the inspiration – often with others – before moving forward in the design process.

You will need to make copies of the previous pages of sketchbook work and this will allow you to cut and paste the best elements together into new juxtaposing or cross-referenced spreads.

Make sure that you have images and fabric swatches that tell the story of the research so far. Colour, texture, shape and details are all important foundations for good design and this exercise is designed to get you to consider the elements that you have found and perhaps also to review what might still be missing, or require further investigation.

The focus pages you create can point to different directions and possible combinations that might arise from your research, and don't necessarily need to be similar depending on how broad and diverse your research has been. But the focus pages will at least help to draw in the key elements that you will need to move the research and design process forward.

Remember: while these pages are designed to form a rough and experimental part of the sketchbook, they can lead into more refined mood- or storyboards, as we will see on the following pages.

Mood-, story- and concept-boards are a way of presenting focused design information to others, whether they be your clients, financial backers, a team of designers or your tutors.

These boards can be described as the front cover to your collection and should tell the story of your research by presenting a few selected pieces of information. Their very name suggests what they are trying to do – that is, to create a mood, tell a story and explore a concept.

Market

Right at the start of your research, you should have considered who you are designing for as a result of the brief you are answering. In terms of the moodboard, it would be important to suggest the client in the images; in other words, to present images that might reflect their perceived lifestyle or to simply use the brand's logo.

Making a board of your own

Mood-, story- or concept-boards are generally presented on board, pinboard or mount card, as this is a durable format.

The size will be dependent on the use, as they are often large scale when used in a design studio, but could be smaller for academic purposes.

The simple layout and composition of images and fabric swatches is all that is needed, and you can even use the techniques explored in research collation as a way of presenting ideas, for example, collage and juxtaposition (seen earlier in this chapter).

◐◑ Examples of moodboards and storyboards.

Styling imagery

This is very closely linked to the market as styling imagery helps to present your designs within a lifestyle context. Selected images can bring an ideal character to the collection. But styling imagery also presents a whole package; the environment or landscape that the photograph has been taken in, the colours, props and styling, hair and make up – all may well contribute to creating an ideal image for your collection.

Key elements

The key elements that a moodboard should contain are:

Colour palette

Colours need to be clearly identified through the use of swatches of colour. These can be paint shade cards, Pantone shade cards or could be mixed by you. It is important to present an image that complements and supports the colours that you have selected.

Reference to theme/research

This is to show the viewer where you have come from in the journey of your research. It needs to focus and edit back to the most important images used for your inspiration; for example, if you have explored styles from the 1920s then there should be images that suggest this.

Fabric

During the research process, you should have begun to collect fabric swatches and ideas for print, embellishment and trims, etc. The moodboard needs to have suggested samples on it to support the developing ideas.

Key words and text

It often helps to have descriptive words or short paragraphs of text that help to describe the theme or story of the collection.

There are no hard-and-fast rules on how to lay out your research in your sketchbook. You do not need to cover every part of the page with your research and drawings; often the negative space adds to the dynamism of a page and how it is read. Different edges and irregular sizes can all add to the composition and layout of the information. Allow the different sources to interact through collage, but also have space in the juxtaposition layout.

Often a wonderful drawing and a single photograph is all that is needed across a double page to explain an idea and present something visually stimulating. The sketchbook should be about balance and so can have both quiet and busy moments in terms of information and sources of inspiration.

Ultimately, the sketchbook is about inspiration and exploration, so it should never be so preciously laid out as to restrict these essential practices. Here are some examples of different sketchbook pages that explore further the ideas discussed in this chapter.

◖◗◖ Student sketchbooks showing various forms of layout and composition, as well as early exploratory design analysis, sketching and use of collage.

Coral Peach Rose Blush Powder Pink

Layering of fabrics

PLEATS

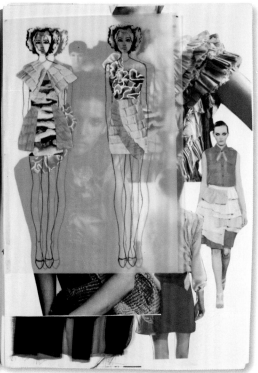

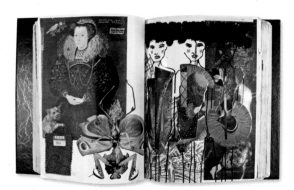

◗◗◗◗ **Further examples of sketchbooks showing early exploratory design analysis.**

INUIT CLOTHING

'fur' hood· inspired by Inuit clothing

Native Arctic prints line hemlines necklines

Beautiful ideas for print and beading

more on shape pri

could be print or embellishment.

graphic print.

Coats made from skins such as reindeer, caribou and polar bear

PRINT IDEAS

Applique on seal skin, 'Human and Animal,' 1956

IDEAS

FOR

TRIMMINGS

↳ Hand stencilled birds on fabric - A traditional. Inuit style print.

Black/Red Printed cotton.

'Dogs see the Spirits' - stencil made by Inuit woman. Many Inuit when they see a dog jump up from a sound sleep and bark, believe that the dog has seen something could be the spirits ....

H
A
N
D
M
A
D
E

E
S
K
I
M
O

P
R
I
N
T

LAZER
CUT....

These bird stencils could be lazer cut of of garments to create a print design.

Omar Kashoura

Of Arabic and English heritage, Omar Kashoura graduated in 2004 with first class honours from the London College of Fashion, and a collection that secured Best International Menswear Designer at New York's Gen Art Style Awards in 2005. He began his working career at London-based fashion house Preen and later Unconditional. In 2006, he completed his Masters Degree at Central Saint Martin's School of Art and Design.

The Omar Kashoura label has since developed into an easily recognizable brand, and has gone on to gain support from the Centre for Fashion Enterprise. In 2008, he won the prestigious Deutsche Bank Pyramid Award and has been awarded BFC NewGen support two seasons running. 2010 saw the launch of a collaboration with the Turkish brand Tween, picked up by Harvery Nichols, Flannels and key stores worldwide. 2012 will see the launch of a designer collaboration with Topman under LENS.

How do you start the research process?

The start of our research comes from a clear headspace. It's an organic moment that happens when it's ready to. To initiate the spark I must have a fresh, undisturbed and open mind. The design research begins and is inspired by circumstance, situations in life that encourage me to question. I am much more inspired by words and feelings. These questions lead me to subjects and through research to events, artists and images, which form the basis for the collection's research.

What kind of brief/constraints/ direction/market do you work to/?

It is vital to consider your market and customer whilst developing your ideas. Menswear is much more product-driven and whilst we may have a great idea or design technique, it has to work within a product which is commercially viable.

Our product sits in the high-end market alongside Burberry and Dries van Noten. Precision is vital for us to compete with the luxury brands and since all our production is managed in the United Kingdom we must devote a lot of time to the technology of a garment, developing internal and external finishing and techniques to each fabric group we work with in each style.

Do you set themes? If so how and where do these start?

The turnaround time from season to season grows shorter. I believe that ideas and design must be developed continuously and not re-invented too quickly. With this in mind we like to carry on thoughts, feelings and sometimes some ideas from season to season. Each season will tell a story and to this we write a narrative. As a person and as a designer I like reason. I like to feel a purpose and to understand cause.

◐◑ Cloth and colour swatches for the 'Love Store' Spring 2012 collection by Omar Kashoura.

What are your sources of inspiration?

Inspiration comes from a few areas: the men who we are designing for and who we aspire to, a theme/concept which creates the mood and then sub-concepts which arrive through initial research which link artists, events, other designers and textiles. When we think of 'the man', we look to masculinity. I am inspired by tradition, by morals and by strength. Images of the classic man in a modern world. Grown up, sexy, robust.

How important is the research to the design process?

Research is vital to our design process. It is one of the most enjoyable parts to the process and each season we learn something new. From initial idea through to the final sample being made for the show is an incredible journey. One which involves a lot of squeezing of the brain, problem solving, and development to get to the final stage.

Whilst we live in a visual world, for me reading literature, history and understanding theory opens the mind. It allows me to imagine and consider. This leads me to images, and page after page of initial ideas in written form.

As a designer, I use my clothes to paint my image of my man, my idea of male beauty. Each season, we develop our own wallpaper of images which cover the studio; they evoke feelings and an energy that will eventually come through in the clothes.

What advice would you give to anyone interested in a career in fashion/ fashion forecasting

My advice would be to live life and experience everything. Own your own identity. Understand rules but develop your own.

Jenny Packham

A graduate from Central Saint Martins College of Art, UK, Jenny Packham's clientele includes the Duchess of Cambridge, Angelina Jolie, Cameron Diaz, Sandra Bullock, Reese Witherspoon, Jennifer Lopez, Jessica Biel, Keira Knightley and Jennifer Aniston.

Her designs are selected for Oscar-nominated film and TV productions, from *Sex and the City* and *The Devil Wears Prada* to the James Bond films *Casino Royale* and *Die Another Day*, to Emma Watson's character in *Harry Potter*.

Her collections feature in some of the world's most discerning stores, from Harrods to Bergdorf Goodman. Heralded as one of the UK's most highly regarded designers, she combines creative talent and commercial success.

Jenny Packham also received the award for Best Bridal Designer of the Year presented by Bridal Buyer in 2011.

How do you start the research process?

Each season is different. Sometimes the inspiration is taken from a trip or a book, a gallery, colours, or even a quote. Knowing what is happening in the market is essential and I always visit the showroom during the selling season to hear the customer's comments. Studying the sales reports and understanding the buying patterns, factoring in economic and political situations, this all affects the following season. It is also important and helpful to have knowledge of the whole season, other designers' collections and of how they were reviewed. Unfortunately, despite all this, fashion cannot be treated as a science and instincts play a large part in planning and creating a collection.

What kind of brief/constraints/direction/market do you work to?

We produce a collection of about 70 pieces per season and have a range of price points to work to. The pre-collection is much more commercial and as we progress to the show we are able to design more freely. We are an international business so there are differences in style globally which we adhere to.

Do you set themes? If so, how and where do these start?

The clearer the idea and the more research accomplished, the easier it is to design. We spend a fair amount of time putting the ideas together and then let them evolve naturally throughout the season.

What are your sources of inspiration?

I love finding points of inspiration. Usually, I have a feeling for the new collection whilst completing the previous one. This is good as it is often when as a team we are most creative. I generally take a few days out to think about how I see the next collection and then we research and create our boards of ideas.

Do you have sources that you repeat or revisit in seasons or collections?

Yes, as one's mood changes something or somewhere that was of little interest before can be right for the moment. Just being in a place that you love or that inspires you can promote creativity. For example… wandering around the Rodin Museum in Paris may not directly inspire a collection but the passion in the work can ignite ideas.

What advice would you give to anyone interested in a career in fashion/ fashion forecasting?

Personally I love what I do; the sketching, the researching, working with pattern cutters and other creative people. I enjoy the business challenges and being involved in promoting and completing sales. I have never wanted to be in fashion for the lifestyle, the parties and the peripheral social scene. If you want to be in fashion for more than a second or two you must have a genuine passion for the process and be willing to be relentlessly ambitious and willing to evolve constantly. If it becomes dull and repetitive you are in trouble.

◖ **Jenny Packham, A/W09.**
Catwalking.com

◖◗ **Jenny Packham, A/W10 (overleaf, left).**
Catwalking.com

◖◗◗ **Jenny Packham, A/W10 (overleaf, right).**
Catwalking.com

Interview: Omar Kashoura > Interview: Jenny Packham

Fashion is a form of ugliness so intolerable that we have to alter it every six months.

Oscar Wilde

4

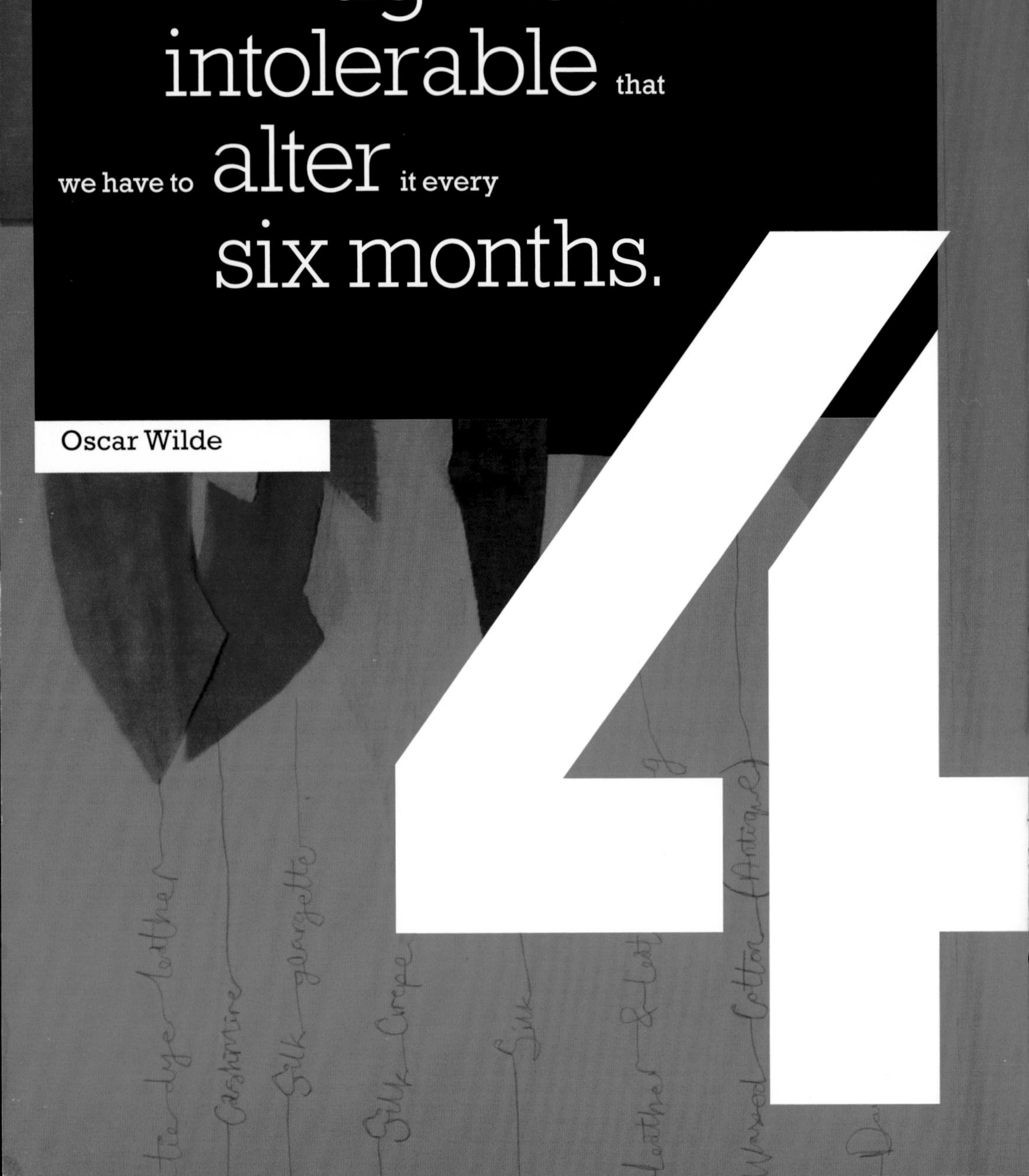

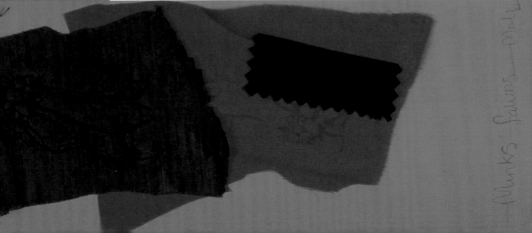

Designing is about mixing up known elements in new and exciting ways in order to create fresh and original products. It is also about exploiting the full potential from the in-depth research gathered and translating this successfully. In this chapter, we aim to explain the fundamental stages of translating research into design. Understanding what the design development processes are and how they affect the creative outcomes is essential to being a successful fashion designer.

We will explore how you can translate early ideas from your research into shapes and structures on the body, using model and drape techniques. As we move into the area of garment development and design, it is essential that you have a basic understanding of fabric and its different qualities. This chapter will further explore the silhouette and function of a garment and look at the use of colour and print. It will also provide you with several exercises to help you to generate design ideas and evolve a collection. The final stages of the design process will be to refine and edit your ideas to create a cohesive and complete collection.

So far, all the work you have explored has been focused on the research and inspiration for the design process, gathering ideas and experimenting with information in your sketchbooks. But what about the design? How do you start to design and to bridge the gap between the inspiration and the actual design process?

Certainly, working on the stand using recycled garments and the model-and-drape technique (see pages 114–115) will provide you with some key ideas for shape and silhouette that can be used in the early translation of research into design. But there are two other approaches that you should also consider to help you to bridge the gap and start the design process. These are collaged research on figures (page 113) and photomontage with drapery (see pages 116–117).

Layout paper

This is slightly transparent paper that can be used with templates to draw design development ideas quickly, so you can trace off the figure easily each time and overlay other ideas. It does not work well with wet media, however, as it tends to buckle.

○○ Student research sketchbooks showing collage on figure.

Collaged research on figures

This is a very quick and quite literal way to translate your research into design ideas and not one that is really used in industry very often, but it is an ideal technique to try as a novice designer.

It will require you to make several copies of different pages of your research, so use a photocopier or scanner to help you at this stage. You will then need to draw out a series of fashion figures or templates (discussed in chapter 5) onto layout paper or directly into your sketchbook. You can then begin to simply cut and collage different aspects of your photocopied research directly on to the figures. This technique allows you to immediately see the design potential of some of the images. Perhaps spiral shells translate into the shape of a skirt or floral leaves into a dress, for instance.

The technique does require you to consider several anchor points on the body, which you will need to start developing your collages from. These are:

- neck
- shoulders
- bust
- waist
- hips.

Arms and legs (that is, sleeves and trousers) should also be given consideration as points to develop from.

This technique concentrates essentially on the possibilities of shapes and silhouettes on the body, but may also suggest colour, print and texture depending on the research images used in this process.

Model and drape is a process of creating patterns and garment shapes through manipulating fabric on the stand or mannequin. Folding, pleating, gathering and draping a fabric on to a three-dimensional stand allows a designer to work on more complex shapes and techniques that are often too difficult to develop in the more conventional manner of flat pattern cutting. Draping fabric does not require the aid of a pattern to create designs, but you can choose to incorporate part of an existing pattern in the preparation.

Draping on the stand

Draping fabric at this stage of the design process is a wonderful way to start early translation of ideas gathered through your research. Taking abstract shapes from what has inspired you and exploring the potential on a mannequin is a much more expressive way of developing ideas for garments than drawing alone, it can be described as akin to sculpting fabric on to the body.

Draping on the stand is also a technique that can help you begin to understand the relationships between a research sketch and a three-dimensional form. It is often difficult to see how a two-dimensional drawing will translate onto the body, so modelling on a stand can begin to explore the idea more clearly.

It is important when using this technique to still be aware of the body and how the fabric relates to it: volume and shape are important, but does the shape flatter the natural contours of the body?

Volume

In fashion terms, this relates to excess fabric in a garment; a garment said to have volume often moves away from the natural curves of the body, creating new silhouettes.

Recording the work on the stand is equally important. Drawing and photographing the ideas as they grow and change is an integral part of the early stages of research and design development and should form an important part of the design aspect of the sketchbook.

By its very definition, draping is about fabric, folds and movement, so it is essential that you have a basic understanding of a fabric's qualities and characteristics. The quality, weight, structure and handle all play an important part in how something looks and reacts on the stand in the model-and-drape process, as we will explore later in this chapter.

Designing from your research

'It's more like engineering than anything else. It's finding the limits of what you can do when wrapping the body in fabric. Everything evolves. Nothing is strictly defined.'
John Galliano
Galliano, Colin McDowell

○ Viktor & Rolf, Knots, 1998 dress, S/S98. In this picture, you can clearly see how modelling and draping techniques have inspired this dress.
Groninger Museum

○ Student toile further demonstrating the use of gathers and draping on the stand.

○ Student sketchbook exploring model-and-drape techniques and development into early design sketching.

This technique expands on the three-dimensional experiments that you began to explore on the stand. The photographs and drawings of these experiments can now be used on a two-dimensional figure in your sketchbook.

You will need to use fashion figure templates again and either layout paper or pages in your sketchbook. This time, instead of using images from your research to collage on to figures you will use the photographs and drawings that you made of drapery on the stand. Try to move the images around the figure and change the scale and placement. Repeating images on the same figure can also be a successful way of gaining further design ideas from your initial experiments on the stand.

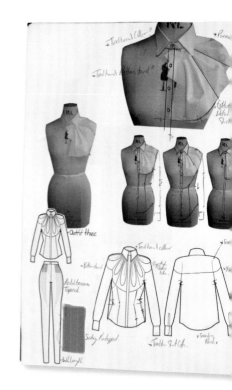

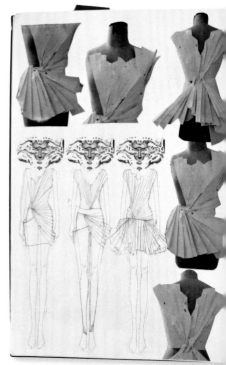

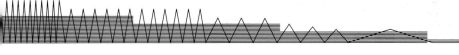

Drawing on to the photomontage figures can add greater depth and may open up other avenues as to the eventual design outcome. You will still need to consider the same anchor points on the body for this technique.

Both techniques of collaging the research directly and working with photographs of draped stand-work can then be worked further into early design ideas by redrawing and refining the garments using layout paper or sketchbook pages.

You should now be well underway with your first design ideas and successfully bridging the gap between the research process and the design process.

⬤⬤ ⬤ Student sketchbooks exploring design drawing from photographs of modelled stand-work and photographic montage techniques.

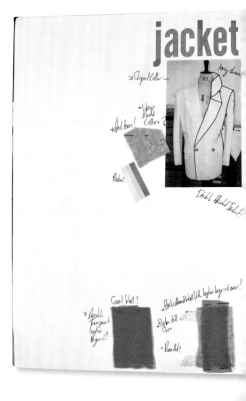

As already discussed, research is guided through a set of required elements or components, which you must consider and gather information for: components such as shape and structure, texture and colour, and historical influences, for example.

It is these elements that now become essential in developing your ideas into garment shapes and details, determining fabric qualities, the use of colour and print, and the creative direction that the collection is ultimately going to take.

There is perhaps also an order that you should begin to consider these elements in as part of the design process. By exploring all of them, you will achieve a greater and more in-depth understanding of your collection and the concept that you have developed.

Design elements

- Silhouette
- Proportion and line
- Function
- Details
- Colour
- Fabric
- Print and embellishment
- Historic references
- Contemporary trends
- Market, levels and genres in fashion

Silhouette

The silhouette of a garment is often the first thing that the viewer will see and respond to when the garment is presented down the catwalk. Silhouette simply means the outline or shape that is cast around the body by a garment.

It is something that is essential to the development of a collection and needs to be seen from a distance before the details, fabric or texture can be discerned.

Closely allied with silhouette is volume. The fullness, bulk or lack of it is readily seen in a garment style and its silhouette. A garment can also contain qualities of lightness or weight through the use of padded, heavy or sheer fabrics, which will again affect the silhouette achieved.

When designing the silhouette, try to consider the garment from all angles (360 degrees) as the silhouette may not be obvious from the first front-view impression.

Developing and refining a silhouette is important to the whole process of design as it will unify and help create an identity for your collection. Inspiration for the silhouette should come from the different elements of your research, specifically shapes and structures or perhaps from historical dress. Looking at abstract shapes in your research and then applying them to a figure is the first stage of basic design development.

Designing from your research

○ **John Paul Gaultier haute couture A/W10 showing a striking shoulder silhouette.**
Catwalking.com

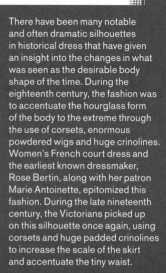

○ **Christian Dior HC S/S11.**
New Look inspired silhouette.
Catwalking.com

○ **Michael Kors S/S11**
asymmetric bias-cut silk dress.
Catwalking.com

Historical silhouettes

There have been many notable and often dramatic silhouettes in historical dress that have given an insight into the changes in what was seen as the desirable body shape of the time. During the eighteenth century, the fashion was to accentuate the hourglass form of the body to the extreme through the use of corsets, enormous powdered wigs and huge crinolines. Women's French court dress and the earliest known dressmaker, Rose Bertin, along with her patron Marie Antoinette, epitomized this fashion. During the late nineteenth century, the Victorians picked up on this silhouette once again, using corsets and huge padded crinolines to increase the scale of the skirt and accentuate the tiny waist.

Christian Dior shocked the world after the Second World War with his New Look in 1947. The collection reintroduced the nipped in waist and gathered full skirt, used much more luxurious fabrics and was a move away from the more austere fashions of the war period and the rationing it brought. The second half of the twentieth century brought hem lines up and exposing legs became much more acceptable; the 1960s' designer Mary Quant created the mini skirt and as they had in the 1920s, women subverted the fashion for the hourglass silhouette and wore their hair short and flattened their busts.

More recently, designers such as Viktor & Rolf, Comme des Garçons and Gareth Pugh have played with the use of scale and proportion in their silhouettes, often moving away from the traditional aesthetics of the body's shape. Their work can be linked more closely with sculptural, even architectural, forms.

Designing from your research

Proportion and line

The proportion of a garment refers to how the body is divided up, either through lines – horizontal, vertical or curved – or through the use of blocks of colour or texture and fabric. The combination of these elements can create infinite and diverse possibilities.

The proportions of the body can be seen through the changes in waist, hem and necklines, and are often judged by the client on their own personal view of their bodies and what suits their body shape.

The line of a garment generally relates to its cut and the placement of seams and darts. These can create visually interesting effects, such as lengthening the body or giving the illusion of a narrower waist. The empire line from the late-eighteenth century raised the waistline under the bust and gave the illusion of a lengthened body.

Bias cut

This is when you cut or drape a fabric on a 45-degree angle to the selvedge, or the horizontal or vertical woven threads called 'the straight of grain'.

Rules of proportion / line

1 Vertical lines tend to lengthen the body.

2 Horizontal lines widen the body.

3 Curved lines or lines cut on the bias will create a more curvaceous and feminine look.

4 Straight lines tend to be seen as more masculine and structured.

5 Seams and darts are not standard and can be moved around the body.

**○ Classic Burberry
trenchcoat A/W11 updated
in orange wool felt.**
Catwalking.com

Function

The function of a garment refers to what
it is: a dress, a skirt, trousers or perhaps
a jacket. The brief you are working towards
will often give you guidelines as to what
is expected at the end of the design process,
so it is important that you are clear on
what types of garments you are designing.

Function can also relate to garments that
have a purpose and specific demands;
for example, garments for the sportswear
industry will need to consider performance,
fabric qualities and the type of sport they
are to be worn for. It is important at the
design stage to know what types of garments
you are designing and what purpose they
need to serve.

Types of detailing

- Topstitching and different methods of stitching
- Fastenings: zips, buttons, hook and eye, eyelets, lace up, straps, Velcro, poppers
- Collar, lapel and cuff styles
- Yoke shapes
- Sleeve shapes
- Dress straps and necklines
- Pocket styles
- Belts
- Finishing of seams, bound, French, channel

Details

A garment can have a wonderful silhouette and good line, but it will be the details that define and differentiate it from other designers' work. The details are what will often clinch a sale. As the client inspects the garment more closely, they are able to see more than just the shape and cut, such as interesting fastenings, topstitching, unusual pockets, collar styles and belts. These are all elements to be considered in the design process and will allow you to explore more subtle changes and developments in similar garments in your collection.

The use of clever detailing is often seen and used more widely in menswear, as extreme silhouettes and bold fabrics are less likely to be used to create new and inventive designs for a largely conservative clientele.

A simple exercise you can do to explore this idea of detailing is to start by drawing out six of the same basic shirt shapes. Then explore the possibilities of different detailing and design six different shirts (see the exercise on page 142 to develop this further).

○ Functional details are developed into the design and construction of the garment.
Alexander McQueen A/W11.
Catwalking.com

◊ Prada dress exploring the use of colour, S/S11.
Catwalking.com

Colour

Colour is a fundamental consideration in the design process. It is often the first element that is noticed about a design and influences how that garment or collection is perceived. Colour can often be the starting point of both the design process and of a collection.

Choosing colours, or a palette for a collection, is one of the earliest decisions that you must make as it will often dictate the mood or season you are working towards. It is therefore vital that you have a basic understanding of colour theory and of how colour can be created and coordinated.

Although it is important to understand colour, most designers will not choose their colour palettes or schemes based on theories.

Once you have got to grips with basic colour theory and mixing colour (see the exercise on the facing page), it will be important to reflect on the original sources of inspiration for the direction you take your colour palette in. It may well be that you explore a variety of ideas using different colour combinations before focusing on one group to design with.

Working with the colour wheel

Colour wheel

There are 12 segments of the colour wheel, starting with:

Primary colours
Red, yellow and blue cannot be made by mixing other colours.

Secondary colours
Orange, green and violet are created by mixing two of the primary colours together.

Tertiary colours
Red-orange, orange-yellow, green-yellow, blue-green, violet-blue and red-violet.

Once you have mixed these colours, they will form a circle or wheel as they go around infusing with each other.

Other terminologies used to describe colour are the following:

Tint
A pure colour mixed with white; for example, red and white make pink.

Shade
A pure colour mixed with black; for example, blue and black make navy blue.

Patina
The surface texture of the described colour.

Tone
A general term to describe a tint or shade.

Hue
This describes the position of a colour on the colour wheel.

Complementary colours
These are pairs of colours that appear on opposite sides of the colour wheel, for example, red and green, blue and orange, and yellow and violet.

Analogous colours
Those colours with a common hue that are adjacent on the colour wheel, for example, blue-violet, violet and red-violet.

The colour wheel is an exercise you can try yourself and will help you understand the basics of mixing colour; you will need to have tubes of either watercolour or gouache paint, water, a palette and a fine paintbrush.

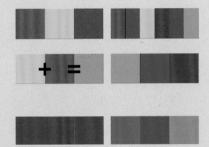

◐ **Examples of primary and secondary colours.**

◐◐ **An example of an analogous colour palette.**

◐◐◐ **An example of a colour wheel.**

⭘ **Pages from a student sketchbook demonstrating an analysis of coloured images.**

⭗ **Missoni S/S11 knitwear demonstrating bold use of colour and pattern.**
Catwalking.com

⭘ **Manish Arora's A/W11 outfit demonstrates a striking use of colour and pattern.**
Catwalking.com

Exercise 5: Working with the colour wheel > **Design development elements** > **Market levels in fashion**

Fabric

The selection of fabric for a garment is often essential to its success. It is both the visual and sensual element of fashion design. The weight and handle of a fabric will determine the way a garment hangs and falls on the body. Designers will often select fabric before designing a garment, gaining inspiration from the way it looks, feels and handles. It may well be that you have sourced interesting textures and swatches of cloth during the research stage and can now start to use them in the development of a collection or garment.

It is important to note that the silhouette is often affected by the quality of the fabric used; for example, a silk jersey will naturally drape and flow around the body, whereas a heavier wool will have more structure and create more volume and shape.

Fabric selection is also about function and performance, in other words, is it fit for the purpose required? For example, denim fabric is used in jeans and workwear because of its hardwearing qualities, whilst Teflon-coated cotton is often used in rainproof sportswear.

Fabrics will often influence the season that is being designed for, as heavier-weight fabrics tend to be used in the autumn/winter and lighter-weights in the spring/summer.

They are also selected for their aesthetic qualities, in other words how they look, feel and support the creative direction you have chosen, whether it be through print, texture or embellishment.

When you start to use fabric in the design process, it is important to source different qualities, weights and types so that you are not limited in the garments that you design.

◖◗ Alexander McQueen S/S11 garment created using digitally printed silk satin.
Catwalking.com

◗ A student sketchbook showing a range of fabric swatches.

'The choice of fabric for a garment is often essential to its success… Fabric selection is also about function and performance, in other words, is it fit for the purpose required?'

○ **Martin Margiela HC A/W10 employing a dramatic use of fur.**
Catwalking.com
◐ **A student moodboard showing swatches of various fabric qualities.**

Designing from your research

Fabric

Fibre

Fibre or yarn is the raw material out of which a textile is created and there are three main categories: animal (protein), vegetable or plant (cellulose) and mineral (synthetics). The fibre or yarn is then used to create fabric through either weaving or knitting it together.

Cellulose fibre

Cotton is a good example of a plant fibre or cellulose fabric. The soft 'cotton-candy' fibre grows around the seed of the plant and is gathered, processed and spun. It has very versatile qualities as it can be woven and knitted and produced in many different weights, for example, denim cotton and cotton voile. It is naturally breathable and absorbs moisture well, which makes it a good cloth for hot climates or the summer season.

◐ **Portobello market fabric stall, London.**

Protein fibre

Protein is an essential component of all living cells and 'Keratin' comes from hair fibres and is the most commonly used protein in the production of textiles.

Sheep and goats are the biggest suppliers of wool fleece, which is the raw product used to create woollen fabrics. Wool is a wonderful warm and slightly elastic fibre that again can be woven or knitted to create cloth. Because of its natural origins it is breathable and durable, and it can also be created in many different weights of cloth for different purposes, from tailored suiting to brushed mohair or angora for knitwear.

Silk is also a fibre derived from an animal, the silkworm. It is collected from the cocoon of the silkworm, which is formed from the continuous thread that it wraps around itself for protection. Due to the way it is harvested, silk has always been a fabric associated with wealth and power. The fibre has lustre to it and can be woven in many different weights and finishes.

Synthetic fibres

These fibres come in two forms, cellulosic and non-cellulosic. The cellulose fibres are created by extracting cellulose from plants and trees and forming fibres such as rayon, Tencel and acetate.

The non-cellulosic fibres are all fibres that are created completely from chemicals and contain no natural fibres. These are known as the synthetics and comprise of fibres such as Lycra, nylon and polyester. The properties that these fibres can bring to fabrics are durability, stretch and water resistance and are often used in sportswear.

They are perhaps best used when they are blended with the natural fibres, such as a polycotton and Lycra and wool together.

Woven fabrics

Woven fabrics are created by interlacing vertical yarns (the warp) with horizontal yarns (the weft) at right angles to each other. The tightness and weight of the cloth will depend on how many threads per centimetre there are and the thickness of the yarn.

Knitted fabrics

Knitted fabrics are formed by linked loops of yarn: horizontal rows are called courses and vertical rows are called wales. The elasticity of knitted or jersey fabric gives good stretch and draping qualities.

Non-woven fabrics

These fabrics are produced by the techniques of bonding and felting. Using heat, compression, friction and chemicals, fabrics are created that do not fray, are waterproof, do not tear and can be recycled. Leather and fur can also be classed as non-woven fabrics although they are not synthetic.

Other fabrics

These cannot be classified in any of the other areas and are essentially craft techniques, such as lace, macramé and crochet.

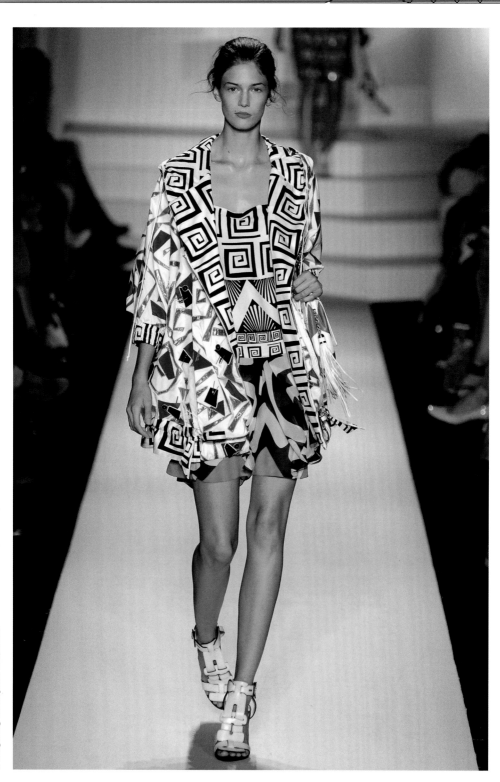

Print and embellishment

Print is a fundamental consideration in the design of a single garment or in the development of a whole collection. Print will often illustrate the colour palette, themes and influences that a designer has been exposed to. Consider a collection inspired by constructivist art and art deco patterns and how these would inform colour and pattern in the garments designed.

Print can be all over the garment in a repeat, it can be a motif in a more considered placement on the garment, or it can be engineered to fit the pattern pieces of the garment. New technologies in digital printing have allowed designers such as Basso & Brooke, Ashish and Mary Katrantzou to fully exploit digital print in their collections and even feature it as their individual selling point, which is one way to stand out in the industry.

We discussed fabric embellishment, such as appliqué, smocking, beading and embroidery, in chapter 1. Embellishment gives a three-dimensional and decorative effect to fabric, and can also help shape or create volume in the garment. Your research might have explored such techniques as sources of inspiration, for example, in early eighteenth century smocking or in African beadwork.

⟡ **Mary Katrantzou S/S11 outfit inspired by Regency interiors.**
Catwalking.com

⟡ **Givenchy HC A/W10 showing beadwork and surface decoration.**
Catwalking.com

⟡⟡ **Diane von Furstenberg S/S11 demonstrating an eclectic use of ethnic and geometric prints.**
Catwalking.com

Historic references

With so much dress history to look at it is no surprise that many designers will look to the past or to other cultures for inspiration. We have already discussed the importance of having an awareness of dress history and how it can provide valuable insight and design details for you to apply to your own creative ideas (see pages 26–27).

Using the information gathered in the research related to historical dress or even perhaps vintage clothing, you can now begin to analyze the elements of design that can be gained from this source; for example, by looking at historical silhouettes, construction details, proportion and line, fabric, print and embellishment. You should now be considering all of these elements in the design of a garment, and exploring a collection in relation to the historical content of your research.

Vivienne Westwood has used direct references to historical silhouettes, garment styles and prints in many of her collections, most famously those based on the archives of The Wallace Collection and the French eighteenth-century aristocracy. She has also drawn inspiration from paintings of period dress, referring to the artist Watteau and the women he painted as a source of inspiration. A slight note of warning should perhaps be sounded: whilst it is important to look at historical and cultural dress and costume, it should not be simply recreated, as to do so would move your work more into the area of costume design than fashion.

Remember: it is about selecting elements of the period source or country of origin and synthesizing them into something new, perhaps by mixing them with other references from your research or by altering the proportions, the placement, the use of fabric or even the gender that the garment was aimed at.

Contemporary trends

We have previously looked at the importance of contemporary trends, through forecasting agencies, global and social interests and even the 'bubble-up' effect from street cultures. The research you have gathered may well contain some of this type of information, and as a designer it is important to have an awareness of what is going on around you and how it may affect your designs and ultimately the client you are creating the garments for.

Using some of the trend information within your design work may well provide useful starting points for some of the design elements, such as colour, fabric or function.

Designing from your research

O Couture Watteau-inspired evening dress by Vivienne Westwood, 1996.
V&A Images/ Victoria and Albert Museum

OO Selection of streetstyle photography by Sarah Mansfield (right, below).

OO Selection of streetstyle photography by Paul Hartnett. Paul Hartnett is a British photographer who has recorded street and club style since the 1970s (bottom row).
© Mr Hartnett / PYMCA

As a fashion designer, it will be essential for you to consider the market that you are designing for and where you see yourself in what is a very diverse and broad-ranging industry. Finding your niche or level will be an important development in your growth as a designer. Therefore, you should understand the different market levels and genres of the industry in order that you can be a more successful designer.

There are essentially two main approaches to garment design and production – haute couture (French for 'high dressmaking') and prêt-à-porter (French for 'ready to wear'). But, as with all industries, these approaches have subdivided over the years into a further series of levels that are more specialist and focused on specific target markets.

◔ Part of the stunningly opulent Christian Dior S/S11 haute couture collection.
Catwalking.com

◔◔ An example of Marc Jacobs's A/W11 ready to wear collection.
Catwalking.com

◔ This outfit by Gucci A/W11 exudes the luxury of this superbrand.
Catwalking.com

Haute couture

Couture is the oldest form of designing and making clothes and was and still is exclusive to Paris, France. The couture fashion shows are held twice a year in Paris, once in January and then again in July. They showcase to the buyers, specially invited clientele and press the absolute top-end, one-off, most expensive, and often most creative and innovative designs that the couture houses have produced.

The industry supports a wealth of amazingly talented and skilled craftspeople from lace makers, beading and embroidery specialists to highly skilled pattern cutters and seamstresses. Some of the most well-known design houses that still produce couture are Christian Dior, Givenchy, Christian Lacroix, Jean Paul Gaultier, Yves Saint Laurent and Versace.

Although there are now very few people across the world who are able to afford haute couture, it still plays a vital role in the industry as it has few constraints on cost and creativity, and is often where ideas and aspirational ideals are first seen before they trickle down into the prêt-à-porter collections.

Ready to wear/prêt-à-porter

The majority of the fashion-buying public cannot afford couture and so the industry has developed a level of fashion called 'ready to wear'. The clothes are still made to a very high standard, but to a set of uniform sizes in much greater quantities. There is still a strong sense of design and innovation, as well as the use of beautiful fabrics and details. There are many more companies working, designing and showing collections all over the world at this level of the industry and, unlike couture, there are more opportunities to show your collections as the ready-to-wear shows are held twice a year in the different fashion capitals of the world, such as Milan, London, New York, Rio, Tokyo and, of course, Paris.

Luxury superbrands

Luxury superbrands are the giant global companies who have huge advertising budgets and are often part of a larger corporation that promotes and designs a wide variety of products throughout their own stores, such as cosmetics, perfumes, accessories and furnishings. The ready-to-wear collections that they show are merely a starting point for the vast sales on additional products that they produce.

The two main contenders at the superbrand level are LVMH (Louis Vuitton Moët Hennessy) and the Gucci Group, who between them own such designer brands as Dior, Celine, Givenchy, Kenzo, Alexander McQueen, Stella McCartney, Marc Jacobs, Balenciaga, Bottega Veneta, Donna Karan, Louis Vuitton and Gucci, to name but a few.

Design development elements > Market levels in fashion > Exercise 6: Design development 1

Mid-level brands and designers

A mid-level brand or designer is an established company with good sales and high profile, but without the power of the superbrands. These brands are often sold through independent design stores or boutiques, department stores and franchises around the world, and they may have their own stores as well. The mid-level designer will generally have a catwalk show and use this to promote a collection to buyers and the press. It is now also the trend for this level of designer to work with high-street brands to create more exclusive ranges based on their own collections, as have Julien Macdonald, Matthew Williamson and John Rocha.

Independent designer labels

The independent designer works with a small team of people to produce a collection. They have total control over the design, sampling, production, promotion and sales. The size of the business will determine how many of these tasks need to be dealt with in-house. The independent designer label will sell wholesale to independent boutiques and department stores and will show through trade fairs and possibly through catwalk shows too.

Casualwear and sportswear brands

Just as with the ready-to-wear designer market, there are superbrands within the more focused fashion design industry surrounding sportswear and casualwear, such as Nike, Reebok and Levi Strauss.

Just as with the superbrands, these niche brands can control a vast global market and can actually influence and impact upon every walk of life. The Nike logo has become one of the most recognized symbols in the world and is not only related to sportswear, but also to a lifestyle. There are also mid-level design brands such as Diesel, Evisu, and G-Star.

High street

The high street has become one of the fastest growing and most diverse marketplaces in fashion design. Companies are able to react quickly to trends on the catwalk because of the way that their design, manufacturing and quality development is set up. Due to the quantities they produce, they can sell at much cheaper prices than designer brands.

The high street in the UK is one of the most directional in the world and stores like Topshop and H&M are fast becoming the favourite places for even the rich and famous to shop at. Equally, places such as large high-street retail stores employ designers like Julien Macdonald and Matthew Williamson to produce exclusive ranges for them and, in doing so, offer that designer's brand name without the designer price tag.

○ A complete menswear collection by menswear designer Oswald Boateng S/S11.
Catwalking.com

'Men's fashions start as sports clothes and progress to great occasions of state. The tailcoat, which started as a hunting coat, is finishing such a journey. The tracksuit is just beginning one.'
Angus McGill
National Geographic
Fashion, Cathy Newman

Womenswear

The womenswear market is the most diverse and directional, as women will purchase clothing much more than men in any one season. Womenswear allows you to be more creative with styles and fabrics and it is seen to be more glamorous. Because of this, it is overly populated with designers and superbrands, so it can be much more difficult to make your own niche or client base within it as a designer. But because of the vast market and variety within it, you are more likely to find employment.

Menswear

This market tends to be more conservative and although there are seasonal ranges, the changes tend to be subtler. Men generally don't buy into as many fashion fads as women and tend to have more classic pieces in their wardrobes. As a result of this, sales in this genre are fewer than in womenswear.

Childrenswear

Childrenswear design can be just as interesting and will often follow similar trends to the main lines. Design brands such as Christian Dior and Versace all do lines in childrenswear. There tends to be more constraints than in the other genres, such as health and safety, and durability and function, especially in relation to clothing created for newborn children and toddlers.

Genres of fashion

There are three genres of fashion that you need to consider as a designer:

1 Womenswear
2 Menswear
3 Childrenswear

...oment 1

...been shown how
...e elements of your
...res to help with
...early brainstorming of ideas. What
this exercise now shows you is how to
get the most from these collaged figures
and how to begin the process of design
development, or collection development.

The collaged figures you produced in
the earlier exercise (on page 111) will have
developed ideas mainly for shape and
some perhaps quite abstract shapes on
the body were explored. What now needs
to be considered is how, through the
addition of these other elements, a series
of related ideas can be developed from
just a few initial collages.

You need to think of design development
as being like a family tree, all the ideas
start from just a handful of key ideas and
through the addition and mixing of other
references and from playing with the
design elements, such as proportion and
line, fabric, print and function, a collection
that has similarities yet differences can
be generated.

Take three collages from the early
brainstorming exercise on figures (they
are labelled A, B, C for this explanation):

A B C

Take each collage and design three
variations of that collage, perhaps
add colour and indicate a print, change
a neckline, add a pocket, change
the function or type of garment. This will
then give you three groups of ideas:

$(A \times 3)$ $(B \times 3)$ $(C \times 3)$

Then from these new ideas that have
similar qualities start to mix across
and see how the best elements from
each grouping can affect the other:

$(AB \times 3)$ $(BC \times 3)$

And then mix once more:

$(ABC \times 3)$

So from the initial three collaged
figures, you have now drawn up 18 further
design ideas and all of them will have
a relationship or similarity to each
other. This is essentially what design
development or collection development
is about – taking a set of known design
elements and mixing them up to create
a series or collection of garments.

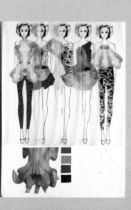

❍ **Student collages developed
into design sketches.**

Designing from your research

Now that the basic understanding of design development has been explained, it is important for you to refine and develop more specific garments from the early experiments you have drawn. The collages and family tree ideas will have begun to explore different combinations of the design elements and hopefully provided you with a set of initial designs.

Refining your collection

You may well have established a strong silhouette or line in some of your work, or perhaps the use of a colour palette or prints was key to their appeal? It is these components that will remain the constant while you develop and further refine the collection.

What this next stage will achieve is to separate out the different types of garments – such as jackets and tailoring, knitwear and jersey, dresses, skirts, trousers, blouses and shirts and outerwear – and begin to focus on the design of variations on these specific types, as a strong collection should contain all of these.

A designer will often have a silhouette and colour palette that is consistent throughout the collection, but by changes in garment type, fabric, use of print and subtle changes to details, he or she is able to create many more outfits in the range.

Coloured Technical Flat Drawings - Final Collection

Final line-up and details - Final Collection

○ **A student sketchbook showing the selection of a colour palette for a collection.**

Design development 2

Identify one garment type from the drawings you have already produced – perhaps a dress, for example.

Take this garment and start to design as many variations as you can – again using the design elements to help you with the development process. Consider changing necklines, hemlines, sleeves, collars, cuffs, fastenings, stitching, use of fabric, pockets, proportions and line, embellishments and the possible use of print.

Remember to stay true to the original idea. This may well have been the silhouette that was created on the body in the initial collages.

You should be able to come up with ten or 20 variations on this one garment and if you then apply this method to all the other garment types you can easily create a set of design developments into the hundreds.

⊙ Student sketchbooks showing design development/ refinement.

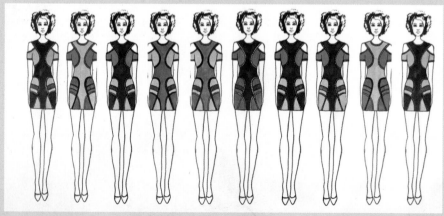

By this stage, you should now have a clear vision operating throughout your designs. The key elements that you have worked with should be apparent and fully explored. Colour, print and fabrics will all have been indicated and considered throughout the process of development and refinement, as well as styles and types of garment.

A good designer will produce hundreds of design sketches, with many variations and subtle detail changes and will then have the task of selecting the strongest ideas to take forward into the final collection edit. It is this stage of the development process that is crucial to the overall success of a collection, as you will need to edit back your designs to create a coherent, well-balanced and harmonious collection.

○ A final student collection design line up.

Unifying your collection

Identify the key pieces or your favourite elements of the collection: is this the dresses, tailoring, jersey or knitwear, skirts, shorts, trousers, jackets or outerwear? Initially, try to build on one piece for each of these types, although it may depend on the season as to the types of garments that are expected in the collection. You don't see swimwear in autumn/winter collections, for instance!

From these key pieces you will need to add in any other important design ideas, for instance the same jacket or dress, but created in several different fabrics. Print often plays a key role in the unifying of a collection and is generally seen in several incarnations, in a dress, a skirt and a blouse, for example.

The portrayal of a silhouette is key to the harmony of a collection and can be seen in many different garments, as can the details placed on them. These elements will create running themes in the final edit and help to establish the final look of the collection.

How many pieces or outfits should be in a collection? This really depends on the size of the design company or budget, as the next stage of the process is pattern cutting, sampling and manufacturing and an independent label may only have the resources to create 20 outfits in any one season, whereas Gucci or Christian Dior may have over 50–80 outfits in their catwalk presentations and the money and manufacturing to support these. As a new designer, you will probably be creating collections of between eight to ten outfits.

WGSN is the leading online trend-analysis and research service providing creative and business intelligence for the apparel, style, design and retail industries.

WGSN's 300-strong editorial and design staff, noted for its significant industry experience, continually travel the globe to deliver insight and creative inspiration, real-time retail coverage, seasonal trend analysis, consumer research and business information.

Complemented by a worldwide network of expert freelance analysts, researchers and journalists, the content staff are the hallmark of WGSN and the foundation of its status as the foremost provider of strategic information.

Launched in 1998, WGSN now has regional offices throughout Europe, Asia, South America and the United States.

How do you start the research process?

We start very broadly. Every season, nearly 100 people from across our global offices compile research on what they think will be relevant in two years' time. These ideas are distilled down into three overarching seasonal themes, or 'macro trends'. At this stage, the concepts are on a cultural-trends level, relating to art and design, film and photography, music, architecture, technology and consumer behaviour, as well as specific product examples of directional fashion.

What kind of brief/constraints/directions/markets do you work to?

Because our client base is global and diverse across all market segments, we need to ensure that we balance our content to the right mix of information, analysis and inspiration. Our schedules are linked to events like fashion weeks, trade shows and the product-development cycles.

Are the creative themes developed as a team? If so, who does what and how does it get collated?

The whole process is based on teamwork. There is a core team to guide the macro trends process, and around that there are temporary work-groups made up of experienced analysts and designers across the content area. The product-specific teams consist of specialists from the respective areas. Since we are an online service, all the relevant research is eventually turned into a digital format, but for meetings and discussions, moodboards are still the medium of choice.

How important is the research to the design process?

Immensely important. There are peak times for it but, generally, it never stops. Our audience is so broad. We always need to know what is going on.

Designing from your research

What role does WGSN have in the fashion industry?

WGSN plays an important role by providing expert information and analysis in an easy-to-use format. Many of us previously worked in the industry so we understand the design and development process, we can shape our content in a way that makes it relevant and actionable. As a company, we operate across the whole product cycle, from initial design inspiration through buying and sourcing to in-store visual merchandising and brand building.

How do you predict the trends so far in advance of the season?

It's a combination of straightforward analysis, experience and gut instinct. But it is also about exposure. If you spend a lot of time in the water and watch carefully, you learn how to pick up on the currents.

What advice would you give to anyone interested in a career in fashion/fashion forecasting?

The work we do at WGSN requires the skills of analysts, photographers, designers, ethnographers and journalists, and many of us find ourselves switching between these roles as needed. So versatility counts for a lot. Clear thinking and communication skills are important. Industry experience helps. We always have a number of interns working in our office. I think trying it out is still the best way to find out if a job is right for you.

� A selection of original WGSN CADs, artwork and design assets available to download from the WGSN website.

Selecting ideas to form a collection > Interview: WGSN > Interview: Julien Macdonald

Julien Macdonald

Julien Macdonald studied Fashion Knitwear at The University of Brighton, UK and received his MA at Royal College of Art, London.

Soon after the success of his RCA graduation show in June 1996, his unique talent caught the attention of Karl Lagerfeld and he was appointed head designer of knitwear for Chanel, as well as for the iconic designer's eponymous label Lagerfeld, from 1996 to 1998.

Following on from his position at Chanel and Lagerfeld, Julien started his own label and began to build his reputation as a leading British fashion designer.

International stars including Beyoncé, Kylie Minogue, Naomi Campbell and Cheryl Cole have worn his designs. In 2001, he was named British Fashion Designer of the Year and was appointed as successor to Alexander McQueen as creative director of the renowned French fashion house Givenchy, where he designed six collections a year from haute couture to prêt-à-porter. In 2004, Julien returned to London to concentrate on his own label, which has grown from strength to strength. He was awarded an OBE for his services to the fashion industry in November 2006.

How do you start the research process for a new collection?

Because it is my own company, I am lucky enough to have the freedom to explore and develop my research and ideas without too many constraints. The main thing that I consider is cost. This is one of the most important things to the buyers, as they will not pay more than they have to for certain styles. There is a European guide that all fashion houses go by that sets a maximum price that customers will pay for certain items like a dress. I will sit and discuss with sales what sold well last season and speak with the production team to see if we had any difficulties. And that is really all – from then on, it is very much down to me to decide what I want to achieve with the collection.

What are your sources of inspiration?

I love to travel and when I have the time I will go and visit many of the great museums of the world and see any particular exhibitions that may be being held. I believe it is important to go and visit the different countries where I sell in order that I can better design with them in mind. I love going to the Metropolitan Museum in New York, the Louvre in Paris, and the Victoria and Albert Museum in London. I often get the V&A to open up some of their archives for me so I can view perhaps a Madame Grès dress or an amazing textile. My studio is based in Portobello Road in London and I love to go and see what is in the market on Fridays.

Designing from your research

○ **Julien Macdonald backstage with models.**

I love looking at vintage clothes and, as well as using the V&A, when I can I go to the Angels costume archives on the outskirts of London. This is an amazing place that has thousands of costumes from all the Hollywood films and is used by many designers and couture houses, including Marc Jacobs and Givenchy. It is an expensive resource, but it is vast and diverse in what you can find, from showgirl costumes to Harry Potter costumes.

I love using books and old magazines. I particularly love looking at old Italian and American Vogue magazines from the 1970s. For my summer collection, I was looking at Matisse and his cut-out paintings as inspiration for print; these were then mixed with orchid photographs taken by Robert Mapplethorpe and then digitally manipulated by a print designer.

Do you ever design a collection with one person in mind?

Not really, I think that the idea of designing to a specific muse can be dangerous as you can in fact alienate some of your potential global market. An actress may not be as popular in Dubai as she is in America. And many actresses want the freedom to wear many different designers and not necessarily be locked into a contract with one design house. I do, however, think of people like Marilyn Monroe, who I love, and the glamorous women of that Hollywood age.

Julien Macdonald

◐ **Julien Macdonald A/W11.**
Catwalking.com

Do you set themes to your collections?

I do like to have themes in what I do, but I don't like them to be obvious references as women want clothes that can be worn and not just presented on a catwalk. So if I wanted to do something with Egyptian art, as this is something I love, I would not then want to style it in that way.

How do you collate your research?

I tend to have storyboards in my studio and these are normally grouped, so I will have inspiration for jersey pieces and then a story for chiffons, dresses and tailoring. There is always a reference for print as this is really the most important part of the collection, as this will often lead all of the design.

How do you start the design process from the research?

The factory will often give me very specific requirements on what they want to see, for example, three dresses, one long, two short, a satin skirt, four blouses and so on, and so from this checklist I can begin to explore ideas within the collection. I do a series of preliminary sketches for each of the storyboards and then from these pick up on running themes or techniques, such as a beautiful idea for embroidery or technical detail that can be developed through several garments in a variety of ways or colours. I very rarely work on the stand, but will develop ideas further when I do the fittings and sometimes will change the look of a garment completely at this stage.

◑◔ **Julien Macdonald A/W11.**
Catwalking.com

Fashion **illustration**
is one **art** form
interpreted by another.

David Downton

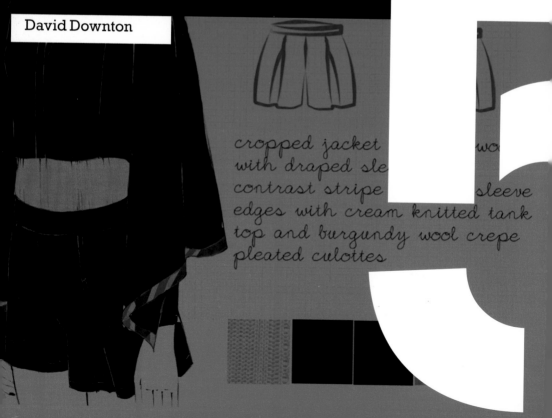

cropped jacket ___ wo___
with draped sle___
contrast stripe ___ sleeve
edges with cream knitted tank
top and burgundy wool crepe
pleated culottes

The ability to communicate your ideas and getting what is in your head down onto paper is an essential part of being a fashion designer. In this chapter, we will discuss the various approaches that you can use to render your ideas and designs, and also explore the use of mixed media and art materials, as well as how they can be used to illustrate different fabric qualities.

Design sketching is only one aspect of fashion drawing and the chapter also analyzes the function of working drawings and the use of templates. Finally, fashion illustration and the role it plays in the industry is explored.

The ability to communicate your thoughts and designs is an essential part of being a fashion designer. Not only is it a part of the development process, but also a way of explaining your thoughts to others. Although it is an important part of the design process, you do not have to be an excellent illustrator or draughtsperson, or even be good at drawing, but obviously it does help.

Having a good understanding of the human anatomy, for example, muscular shapes, proportion, balance, stance and skeletal structure, will assist in the ability to draw and ultimately design more convincingly. One way you can develop this skill is to attend life-drawing classes, which are often run as evening classes at your local college or adult education centre.

○ ○ Sketchbook examples of design sketching, incorporating textiles and further details of construction.

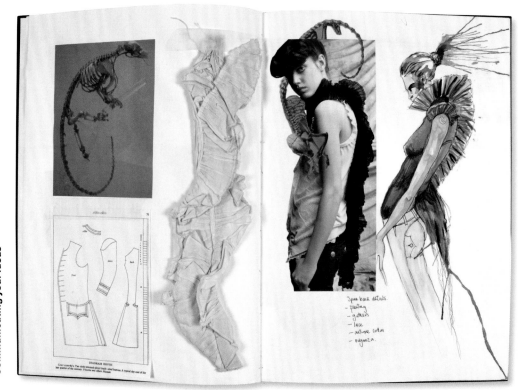

'I don't design clothes.
I design dreams.'
Ralph Lauren

Mastering your style through sketching

Another approach to developing your drawing is to sketch people on the move, perhaps walking past a café, on the subway or in the street. Capturing people in motion and seeing how their clothes move and respond to the body is also an important part of understanding how fashion can be drawn.

In academic schools, fashion drawing and sketching is often given a lot of time and attention as the ability to visually describe your designs and develop them through drawing with originality and personality is one of the fundamental parts of the design process. The design sketch must be figurative (in other words, it must vaguely resemble the human form), although it can be stylized and stretched to some extent. Long legs are an aesthetic to consider, as catwalk models tend to have long legs.

The sketch needs to describe the key design elements; therefore, it is important to draw not only the silhouette, but also the garment details, fabrics, print ideas and colours. It is the main tool used in exploring ideas; rendering the figure many times over will allow you to play with the design elements in different combinations.

The design sketch itself should be something that is quick and allows you to get your ideas down rapidly. The mind can move very quickly and wander off into different directions as you get more inspired by the research you have gathered. Speed often provides spontaneity and energy to your design work. Mastering your own style will also present uniqueness to your designs and add to the identity of the work.

Having basic skills in figure drawing and mark-making will always assist in the speed and accuracy of your rendered design work, but one tool that can help with this process is a fashion template.

Mark-making

Mark-making is the name given to the practice of using different art media and the methods of putting marks on to paper in a creative and expressionistic way.

Fashion templates are pre-drawn figures that can be used by tracing them off through layout paper or tracing paper and then drawing designs over the top. Templates allow you to focus on the design work and not on the figure. They also allow you to work quickly and in a more repetitive manner, perhaps working on the same type of garment many times until the strongest design appears.

Templates can be found in most illustration fashion books, but where possible it is best to try and develop your own figures to work on, as they will be more individual and help you develop your own style and hand in fashion figure drawing.

The example below illustrates the development of a fashion figure through the different stages of development: from initially mapping out the proportions of the head, shoulders, waist and legs to marking in the figure, then the garment shapes and details, and eventually the colour and texture of the fabrics.

◡ Here you can see how a basic design template is developed through a series of stages, considering proportion, balance, garment shape, colour and fabric rendering.

Creating a design development six-figure template

As a designer, it is essential that you develop and perfect your own style of rendering your design ideas, and create a template that allows you to work quickly and able to communicate specific garments or details to others effectively.

Templates can be developed from life drawing, but you can also use collage and pencil outlines from magazine images. You will now create a line up of six figures on an A3 landscape piece of paper. Why six? Well, you generally develop ideas across a mini-collection of six outfits, so the ability to see all six outfits at once is essential to the selection of a cohesive and balanced collection. You should never really design develop an idea in isolation with only single figures.

You will need: a retractable pencil; tracing paper; scissors; a glue stick; photocopies from fashion magazines/ catwalking shots and access to a photocopier or computer with Photoshop software.

Firstly, source some head-to-toe figures – preferably catwalk-type images – that give you front-on views. Look for back views too. Once you have found a good image, trace around the figure using a pencil and tracing pad, getting as much detail of the silhouette, face, hands and shoes as you can, but without too much detail of the clothes at this stage. An image from a swimsuit collection is ideal, as this shows a lot of the figure with little clothing to distort the body silhouette. This can also be achieved using a scanner and the drawing tool in Photoshop.

Photocopy the original figure, and cut out the of the arms, legs or shoes. Glue these to your drawing (or do this in Photoshop). Stylize the head and face in your own hand, adding a strong individual dynamic through the use of mixed media.

You now have a template with a simple line-drawn outline of the figure, collaged with photographed or drawn stylized head/face/hair/feet/shoes/hands. How much of the original photograph to use is up to you. Photocopy this template five times and stick all the figures side by side on one sheet of A3 landscape paper.

Photocopy this, reducing the contrast of the drawn body-line to a faint outline. Then copy as many figures as you need for drawing and collaging design ideas on top. (Do this using Photoshop and a printer if you wish to incorporate colour into the figure's hair and face.) You can now design directly onto the template, adding garments, details, and simple colour to the figures in flesh tones.

As the outline of the figure is faint, you will not see the lines when drawing garments, but they will help you with proportions and maintaining a standard to the design work developed. These figures can then form the basis of your design development book/sketchbook and can be bound to form a catalogue of design that has been sequenced to develop various garment types, fabric and colour permutations, and outfit combinations.

We have already discussed using collage in both your research and early design work (see pages 86–87), but collage can also be a vital tool in the rendering and illustration of your fashion designs. Working with a variety of mixed media and different paper qualities, in conjunction with components of your research, can provide a very effective and original design sketch.

The use of collage also provides a freer and sometimes more expressive approach to the design process. Collage is best used alongside drawing at this stage, as the details of the garments designed can be lost in the use of large pieces of photographic, perhaps more impressionistic, images.

○ Research is collaged onto the figure to create a more atmospheric and evocative illustration.

pens down,
time's up

cropped jacket in navy wool
with draped sleeves and
contrast stripe trim on sleeve
edges with cream knitted tank
top and burgundy wool crepe
pleated culottes

pens down,
time's up

oversized knitted cardigan in mustard
with printed and embroidered cotton
poplin shirt with pleated bodice and
checked cotton kilt with stripe edge trim

◐◑ Student examples demonstrating the use of collage on figures for illustration and design.

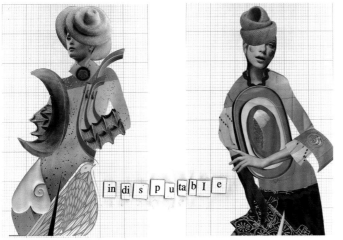

The use of a variety of art materials is important throughout the whole process of research and design as it allows you to explore your own hand and preferred choice of media. It also allows you to illustrate a variety of images and interpret them into new forms, patterns, colours and textures. It is therefore essential that you equip yourself with the basics and understand how they can be used.

Some basic art materials

1 Adhesive glue stick
Glue sticks are dry glue that is particularly useful for sticking paper, as it does not soak through in the same way that PVA glue can. This glue is essential when using collage in your research and also in the experimental design stages. It does not dry immediately on contact and so allows you to reposition images when necessary.

2 Acrylic paint
Acrylic paint is a water-based paint. It will dry with the textures and brush marks created through application. It can have a slightly glossy look and can be used to render plastic and leather garments successfully.

3 Gouache paint
Unlike acrylic paint, gouache will dry flat and even with an opaque finish. It is slightly matt and chalky in finish and allows you to either water it down to get a lighter shade or use it more thickly to get a darker shade. It is a good paint to block in even colour and can be used with other media, such as oil pastels and coloured pencils, to render different textures and fabric qualities.

○ Final design illustrations using mixed media drawing techniques.

Communicating your ideas

4 Watercolour paint

A transparent paint that is used with water. It can be bought in tubes or in solid blocks that can be purchased as sets. It mixes well and takes on the characteristics of the paper it is painted on; for instance, used on coloured paper it will take on the colour of that paper as a tint. It is great for illustrating more sheer and delicate fabrics because of its transparent qualities. Used with plenty of water, it will dilute to very pale and subtle shades. It works best on good quality cartridge or watercolour paper.

5 Water-soluble colouring pencils

These are a quick and easy way to apply and mix colour directly onto your drawings. Used dry they can give the impression of texture and the weave of a fabric, while used with a little water, applied with a brush, they can be mixed to present a more transparent fluid mark.

6 Paintbrushes

Always invest in a good set of brushes in a variety of widths made from natural fibres, such as sable. They will last longer and will not flare after use, which can make accurate painting difficult. Both flat and round heads are useful, as they will allow you to make different types of brush marks and illustrate different details. Always wash your brushes thoroughly after use and remove all residue paint or ink.

7 Magic marker or brush pen

These are superior felt tip pens and come in a huge variety of colours and shades that will often allow you to match up exactly to your colour palette. They will lay down colour evenly and flat and also allow you to build up layers and darker tones. They can be expensive but are well worth the investment as they are the quickest and simplest way to put colour accurately into a design sketch. Marker pens can also be used with other media such as coloured pencils and can often be the base colour to a fabric with pencils providing the texture.

8 Fine-line pen

The fine-line pen comes in a variety of thicknesses and is generally used in the rendering of designs and particularly working drawings, as it gives a precise, graphic and even mark.

9 Retractable pencil and lead

The retractable pencil is a reusable pencil that can have the lead replaced and changed, as it is needed. You can vary the grade, from hard 4H, to soft 3B, depending on your requirements. For design sketching, it is best to have a lead that is anywhere from B to 3B and in the pattern-cutting room, it is better to have a harder lead, H to 3H. The benefits, apart from the ability to change the grade, are that you always have a sharp, precise mark, which is essential in design work.

10 Putty rubber

This is a more mouldable rubber than normal hard erasers. It can therefore be more precise for removing pencil marks and smudges.

11 Pencil sharpener

This is used to sharpen normal pencils and watercolour pencils to achieve a clean, sharp mark on the page.

12 Layout paper

This is a slightly transparent lightweight paper used in the design drawing process. It is perfect for using with templates as they can just be seen through the paper and therefore allow you to trace the figure quickly and easily before applying the design work. You can purchase different types of layout pads; there are some that work well with magic markers and which stop the bleeding through to other pages. As the paper is lightweight, it is not recommended that you use any wet media with it, as it will tend to buckle and disintegrate.

It is important to know the difference between fashion design sketching and illustration, as the two play quite different roles. As discussed earlier in the book, the design sketches are about the clothes; they show the silhouette, details, fabrics, print, embellishments and colour. They are used to describe and show the clothing as it would be worn, they are generally in proportion and they represent a visual tool to help the pattern cutter create the garment. They are also quick and can appear more spontaneous.

Illustration, on the other hand, is seen as an art form in itself, as it allows you to be even more creative with your use of media and the quality of lines or brush marks that are laid out on the paper become more important and influential on the way the garments are perceived. Illustration is about evoking the mood of the collection and need not show the garments in full or even in a way that is obvious as to what they are. The work is much more expressive and stylized and often captures the spirit or even the character or muse that the collection was created for. The wide use of mixed media, digital and Photoshop software can all be explored.

◐ Final collection presentation illustration, using drawing, collage and photoshop.

◑ Student sketchbook showing collaged design drawing.

Working drawings, specs, flats or technical drawings, as they are often referred to, are the diagrammatical detailed drawings of your design work. They are the graphic, clearly drawn explanation of the garment, showing all the construction details, such as seams, darts, pockets, fastenings and topstitching.

Producing your drawings

The flats are drawn with no figure represented, but to scale and as the name suggests in a flat rendering, with no indication of colour, texture or form. They will also show both the front and the back of the garment, something that is often forgotten in the design sketch.

The working drawing is used to support the sometimes more fluid and artistic design sketch and must always be presented with the correct body proportions, as it is generally the drawing that a pattern cutter will interpret a pattern from, as the design sketch can sometimes lead to inaccurate proportions.

A working drawing is generally produced using either fine-liner black pens or a clutch pencil, which uses fine leads. Different widths of fine-liner can be used in the same drawing to illustrate different components, for example, a 0.8mm thick pen can be used for all the seam lines, darts and details, whereas a 0.3mm thick pen can then be used to indicate all the topstitching, buttons and fastenings.

Flats

O Final portfolio working drawing and technical specification sheet. Each garment is clearly represented with both front and back details drawn.

The layout and composition of your work will greatly depend on how you have presented your designs. Most of the work you do will be contained in a sketchbook or on sheets of layout paper; these can then be bound into one presentation. The layout of a design page will often require you to work on figures in a series of groups – three as a minimum and up to six – in a row across the page and generally on A3-sized paper (420 x 297 mm).

This allows you to develop ideas across several figures at the same time and to immediately see any connections, running themes or similarities occurring across the design. The layout therefore becomes much more simplistic and uniform as the design becomes progressively more important, eventually showing just rows of figures with the design applied to them.

The final part of the process

As the design becomes more selected and refined, the figures and their composition can become more complex and creative. As the designs have been edited, you can spend more time on the drawing and rendering of the individual figures and designs. There are no hard-and-fast rules – whether you work in portrait or landscape format is up to you.

Line-ups and groupings of the final collection can be presented in a variety of ways and may be influenced by themes from the research and design process. Using different positions, stances and styles of drawing, perhaps influenced by a period, can all affect the final layout and look of the design work.

Using fashion magazines and photo shoots can help to suggest the positions of a final presentation. Figures sitting, standing next to one another, with one in the distance and one up close – these choices really come down to your own personal preferences.

The composition and layout of these selected designs is the final part of the process, and rendering the design work and considering the format is an important part of presenting this work. The creativity you have developed in the research and design process is now consolidated in the final designs and how you present them. Remember: your final presentation should always be first and foremost about the clothes.

Communicating your ideas

○ **Final design illustrations using traditional drawing methods mixed with the use of Photoshop.**

So far in this book you have learnt all about the importance of research and where and how to collate it, as well as about its purpose in directing the design process.

So what happens next?

As with any product that has been two-dimensionally designed, it is essential that it is realized three-dimensionally so that any further developments and refinements can be completed before it is made up in the actual finished fabric or material. This first make is called a toile or sample. You will need to have a basic knowledge of flat pattern-cutting and garment construction to be able to understand how to transfer shapes and silhouettes onto the body from the design drawings that you have created. It takes designers years to perfect their skills and refine their ability to realize their drawings, so do not be disheartened if it does not work first time around!

You may have already explored some three-dimensional ideas on a dress stand to gather information for designing and these experiments may be a good starting point for pattern development. Modelling on the stand is a great way to learn about body shape and how flat fabric translates into form-fitting garments. Using the experiments can help to define an early paper pattern that can be refined and refitted to the body until it starts to relate to the design drawings that you have created.

Technical drawings are also a good and more precise interpretation of the sketches that you have created in the design process. These are generally what a designer will use to develop the precise paper patterns used in toiling a garment.

Creating your first toile from a design or technical drawing will show you the merits of the shape and details that your garment possesses. These can then be altered and changed as needed, drawing on the toile itself, cutting and adding as needed. These changes can later be corrected on your flat pattern pieces and be subsequently retoiled if necessary. The whole process of moving your flat drawings into three-dimensional garments is fundamental to the success of a fashion designer. Without the understanding of the craft and skills of creating and working with a product, there cannot be a real understanding of how to design effectively.

Taking your designs beyond the drawing board is something that all fashion designers should have a basic and working ability to achieve. Learning about the cut and construction, as well as working with industrial equipment such as sewing machines, overlockers and pressing, will give you a much more confident ability to work within the industry.

'Fashion is about change and about challenging what has gone before; it is about leading and not following; you should never feel that you cannot achieve your goals or push your design vision into the world.'

There are many good classes and self-help books that can guide you through this part of the process and most full-time college and university courses in fashion design will teach you the skills you need as part of the curriculum.

Fashion requires you to have skills and strengths in many varied aspects of the design process; being able to research and collate information is key; processing this information in order to creatively draw and design ideas will need to come naturally over time; considering constraints and problems likely to be faced along the way is an inevitability that you should be prepared not to shy away from. Once you've mastered these strategic elements of the process, you will then have to consider yourself as both a technician and seamstress, and work with equipment and fabric to successfully realize your designs. Gaining all these skills takes designers years to perfect and refine until they reach a point of success and identity in the work they create.

A few final words...

With this book, you have started a journey of discovery, interest and passion; and you now have the insight, skills and knowledge to pursue your dreams. As with all creative endeavours, it will take time for you to perfect your abilities and to discover who you are and what you are about in terms of design.

All the great designers have had a strong personal signature to their work, and this can only be found through experimentation and exploration. Do not restrict yourself and never feel that you have seen and done it all. A good designer will be driven to challenge themselves, to always look for the next new direction, and to constantly seek out further influences and sources of inspiration with which to stimulate their work.

Fashion is about change and about challenging what has gone before; it is about leading and not following; you should never feel that you cannot achieve your goals or push your design vision into the world. A good designer will constantly challenge him or herself, will always look for new directions and seek out further-reaching influences, technologies and sources of inspiration to stimulate and drive their work. Always remember: with practice and experimentation, anything is possible!

Enjoy your future career in fashion and good luck!

David Downton

David Downton graduated in Illustration/Graphics from Wolverhampton Polytechnic in 1981. In 1984, he moved to Brighton and began his illustration career. For the next 12 years, he worked on a wide variety of projects from advertising and packaging to illustrating fiction, cook books and, occasionally, fashion. In 1996, he was commissioned to draw at the couture shows; David has since become known as a fashion illustrator. His reports from the shows have been seen internationally, in the US, China, Australia and the Middle East.

David's client list includes: Tiffany & Co., Bloomingdales, Barneys, Harrods, Topshop, Chanel, Dior, L'Oréal, Vogue, Harper's Bazaar, V Magazine and the V&A Museum. In 1998, he started work on a portfolio of portraits of the world's most beautiful women, including Paloma Picasso, Catherine Deneuve, Linda Evangelista, Carmen Dell'Orefice, Iman and Dita Von Teese. In 2007, David launched Pourquoi Pas? the first ever journal of fashion illustration. He is visiting professor at London College of Fashion, and has an honorary doctorate from the Academy of Art University, San Francisco.

What is fashion illustration?

Fashion illustration is one art form interpreted by another; in other words, it is a designer's vision filtered through an artist's creativity. It absolutely requires you to respect the work of the designer and it should bring out the best of the both of you. When working with haute couture particularly, I am well aware of how much has gone into each of the pieces, having met many of the people involved, and I do feel a real responsibility to attempt to do it justice. I do sometimes feel guilty using such a reductive line to describe something so intricate. Classical illustration such as this, going to view the catwalk presentations and distilling the essence of the shows through drawing, is a rarity now.

Fashion illustration has changed beyond recognition over the last decade. There are no rules, no restrictions and no prescribed way of working. There is no prevalent style and hand-drawn and digitally made imagery have an equal validity today. The market has broadened to embrace club flyers, CD covers, gallery exhibitions, as well as the more traditional outlets of newspapers and magazines. To sum up, I would say there has never been a better or more confusing time to be a fashion illustrator.

◐ ◑ Examples of David Downton's fashion illustrations. These demonstrate more traditional painted qualities and brush-mark techniques.

Communicating your ideas

Caryn Franklin

Caryn Franklin is a British fashion writer, broadcaster and director. She started her career as the fashion editor and co-editor of i-D magazine during the 1980s and has been a fashion commentator for over 29 years. Caryn famously co-hosted the BBC TV show The Clothes Show which ran for 12 years from 1986–98.

Caryn has been an external assessor and lecturer for various UK colleges, including The Royal College of Art, Central Saint Martins and The London College of Fashion.

As a fashion activist, she has co-chaired Fashion Targets Breast Cancer for 15 years. Caryn proposed the Centre of Sustainability at The London College of Fashion and, as one of its ambassadors, promotes ethical sourcing and supply. She also co-founded the award-winning All Walks Beyond the Catwalk (with Debra Bourne and Erin O'Connor), a groundbreaking initiative promoting diverse beauty ideals.

www.allwalks.org

What in your opinion makes a great designer?

A great designer is someone who has empathy with the end usage of the product. Design has to have a purpose – currently, designers create prototypes for the catwalk or to feature in an edgy editorial photograph, but the sample or prototype is just one aspect of the design. Designers who consider the life of the garment when it is duplicated and how it will work on ordinary bodies will not only have a more lucrative business proposition, but will also be embracing the service aspect of what fashion and clothing design is about. Clothes are after all about serving the wearer.

A good design is a piece of creative vision married with technical excellence. When it has heart and soul, and when it can flatter and embolden the wearer, when it is emotionally considerate of the wearer's needs, then it serves its rightful purpose and becomes a piece of design that is fit for purpose.

> 'A good design is a piece of creative vision married with technical excellence.'

Communicating your ideas

⟁ Caryn Franklin and British fashion designer Jeff Banks present awards to students at Graduate Fashion Week, London in 2011.
Catwalking.com

How important is creative research to a designer? and why?

Research is what yields a fresh take and perspective. Research when combined with agenda can be what shines a light on the way forward.

How important is the marketing and promotion of a collection to its success? What would need to be considered by a new designer?

Marketing is everything. Telling people what you do is the only way to bring buyers/consumers to your door – but it is a skill all on its own. For a young designer on a limited budget, the goal is to link up with someone who can manage this aspect independently. Maybe they too are just starting out and can bring the skills they have learned to the table, leaving the designer free to negotiate the design process.

What advice would you give to someone wanting to be a fashion designer, or work in the industry?

Think of fashion design as a profit-making activity, not a wonderful hobby. Everything you do as a student or an apprentice must be about understanding how to earn your living from the skills that you have acquired. With this in mind, you can approach learning in a different way.

Interview: David Downton > Interview: Caryn Franklin

Abstract A concept that describes an idea, feeling or quality; not reality.

Aesthetic An object or design that depicts beauty or pleasing appearance.

Anchor Points Points on the body that a fashion illustrator or designer will use to develop shapes or forms from, such as the neck, shoulders, bust, waist and hips.

Appliqué This is a technique where a piece of cut-out fabric is sewn or fixed ornamentally to another fabric so as to create a surface decoration or pattern.

Beading This is exactly as it sounds, the decoration of fabric with beads, usually sewn.

Brief A set of instructions directed at a designer, to outline the aims, objectives, and final outcomes.

Client-based Describes a product to be designed for a particular company or target market.

Collection A group of garments designed with certain features in common, such as colour or shape.

Commercial Describes a product that is intended to be bought by the general public.

Composition The way that visual elements along with text can be arranged on a page.

Conceptual A vision based on ideas or principles.

Consumer Analysis Collating information about the lifestyle of the target customer group, such as age, economic status and occupation – which helps to guide the designer in creating commercially viable products.

Consumer Behaviour The analysis of consumer lifestyle and spending habits.

Contemporary Existing or happening now.

Contours The surface or shape of a garment or the body formed by its outer edge.

Critical Path The time and process involved in creating a garment or collection, from concept to creation.

Cultural Influences Relating to the habits, traditions and beliefs of a society; or relating to music, art, theatre, literature, etc.

Customization To make or change elements of a garment to individualize the look or style.

Demographics Characteristics of a population regionally or nationally, usually in relation to their age, income and expenditure.

Disparate Different in every way.

Drape Techniques The way in which cloth folds or hangs as it covers the body or mannequin.

Embroidery This is the craft of sewing thread on to the surface of a fabric to create patterns and texture. By using different types of thread and stitch you are able to create elaborate surface decoration on flat fabrics.

Fashion Forecasting The process of predicting forthcoming trends.

Genres Describes a style that involves a particular set of characteristics within a category of, for example, art, literature or music.

Haute Couture Originally a French term, meaning high-fashion, custom-fitted clothing. Literally means 'high dressmaking'.

Journals A magazine or newspaper published about a specialist subject.

Juxtaposition To put things which are not similar next to each other.

Lustre The shiny or bright surface of a fabric.

Mainstream Lifestyle or habits adopted by the majority.

Market The business or trade of a particular product, associated with the sale of products.

Merchandising Department The department responsible for allocating and arranging garments creatively, for example, in window displays.

Motif An identifiable pattern, design or logo.

Muse An imaginary person or icon that gives a designer ideas and helps them to focus.

Narrative A story or a series of events.

Negative Space The space around an object that can be used in composition to balance positive space.

Niche A specialized product group targeting a specific area of the market.

Palette A group of colours that sit well together.

Pantone Internationally recognized numbered shades and colours used throughout the creative industries.

Pop Art A type of modern art that started in the 1960s and uses images and objects from everyday life.

Punk Culture popular among young people, especially in the late 1970s, involving opposition to authority expressed through shocking behaviour, clothes, hair and music.

Season Described in fashion terms as spring/summer or autumn/winter, usually fashion products are designed at least one season ahead.

Sensory Connected with the physical senses of touch, smell, taste, hearing and seeing.

Silhouette The outline shape of a garment or collection.

Smocking This is a technique using stitch to gather fabric in a honeycomb pattern. There are many variations to this basic stitch and it allows the designer to create shape and volume in a garment without the need to cut the fabric.

Subculture A group of people who share similar customs, tastes and ideas in, for example, music.

Surrealist/ism A cultural movement and visual art depicting unusual happenings or events, not based on reality.

Swatches A small piece of cloth used as an example of the colour or texture of fabric or a sample.

Target Market The group of customers that a retailer aims to sell to.

The Bubble-up Effect Fashion seen in street or subculture that influences designer fashion.

Viewfinder A frame that allows you to conceal or expose part of an object or image.

Visual Language An image created to communicate an idea using line, shape, colour, texture, pattern, scale, and/or proportion.

Zeitgeist German expression that means 'the spirit of the times'; a general set of ideas, beliefs or theories.

Color Portfolio

Color Portfolio is a full service colour, trend and communications marketing company. You can buy their colour presentation cards online. They also offer an offline service if you are looking for personalized design and concept development.
www.colorportfolio.com

Cotton Incorporated

Interested in textiles? In cotton? Check out this website for great information. Cotton Incorporated is a research and promotion company aiming to increase the demand for and profitability of cotton by providing value-added programmes and services both in the US and internationally for producers, mills, manufacturers and retailers.
www.cottoninc.com

Ellen Sideri Partnership Inc

Consulting company providing trend analysis, colour forecasting, brand design, retail store design and web consulting.
www.esptrendlab.com

Fashion Information

This subscription-based website is a terrific source for a view of international apparel trends. Reports for subscribers include updated catwalk trends and detailed illustrations, pictures and colour charts.
www.fashioninformation.com

Fashioning an Ethical Industry

Fashioning an Ethical Industry is a Labour Behind the Label project that works with students and tutors on fashion-related courses to give a global overview of the garment industry, raise awareness of current company practices and of initiatives to improve conditions, and to inspire students – as the next generation of industry players – to raise standards for workers in the fashion industry of the future.
http://fashioningan ethicalindustry.org/home/

Fashion Net

This site gives you fashion news, designer bios and runway shows and also has useful links such as fashion sites, online magazines and designer sites… You can buy and sell stuff on this website.
www.fashion.net

Fashion Toolbox

New York based company that develops, publishes and markets design and production software packages for the apparel, textile, accessories and surface design industries. They offer high-end design solutions.
www.fashiontoolbox.com

Fashion Windows

Great site! Extensive listings covering fashion trends, runway shows, fashion reviews, designers and models. Find the latest news and visuals from the fashion world as well as great information about visual merchandizing. Most info available to subscribers only! Easy to use.
www.fashionwindows.com

FutureFrock

Launched in 2009, FutureFrock is a forward-thinking online magazine focusing on one of the industry's most exciting areas, ethical style and beauty. Brought to you by a collective of fashionistas who are passionate about ethics and the environment, FutureFrock doesn't desire to preach or proselytize. Instead, they aim to let the products speak for themselves – and these are gorgeous, cutting-edge and all the more exciting because of their ethical credentials.
http://futurefrock.com

Global-Color

Global-Color is a forecasting company providing solutions to colour selection in the fashion and interiors industries. Great information and inspiration for colour. Easy-to-use format with nice graphics. Their products are available to order online.
www.global-color.com

Le Book

A good sourcebook for trends and inspiration for fashion designers, cosmetic companies, advertising agencies, art directors, magazines, photographers, fashion stylists, make-up artists and hair stylists. It is for sale on the website. There is also a great list of contact names.
www.lebook.com

Moda Italia

Modaitalia.net's fashion search engine helps you to find what you need from the fields of fashion, textiles, beauty and lifestyle.
www.modaitalia.net

modeinfo

This site sells the international trend publications and trade press for the fields of fashion, textiles, interiors and lifestyle as well as books about fashion, and forecasting catalogues and magazines. Also has lists of Pantone products, seminars and international fairs.
www.modeinfo.com

Nelly Rodi

A trend-consulting company focused on colours, fabrics, prints, knits, lingerie, beauty and fashion. Find a list of their trend books on the website. In addition to their trends research, they offer communication services in publishing and organizing events.
www.nellyrodi.com

Pantone Inc.

Nice presentation and easy navigation. Pantone provides colour systems and technology across a variety of industries. They have products such as 'colour matching system', a book of standardized colour in fan format. This is a reference for selecting, specifying, matching and controlling colours in colour-critical industries, including textiles, digital technology and plastics. You can buy everything online.
www.pantone.com

Peclers Paris

The biggest fashion consulting company in Paris offers style and product, promotion and communication consulting. Peclers trend books are very well known but you can't buy them online yet.
www.peclersparis.com

Promostyl

Promostyl is an international design agency researching trends. Find their books and products for sale on their site. They have offices in Paris, London, New York and Tokyo.
www.promostyl.com

Sacha Pacha

A Parisian styling bureau in service of the fashion industry. They offer exclusive collection design and personalized trend consultancy. Find the Sacha Pacha trend books for menswear, womenswear and juniors here.
www.sachapacha.com

Style.com

Too good to be free! This online website features complete fashion shows coverage (the videos and photos are online right after the shows), the lowdown on celebrity style, trend reports, expert advice and breaking fashion news.
www.style.com

Styloko

Styloko is a UK network of sites fanatical about style, fashion and shopping. A team of fashion-obsessed editors find and follow all the global trends, the best styles, deals and products and deliver them in digestible portions. The main aim of this site is to bring global fashion and local UK shopping together.
www.styloko.com/buzz/category/trends/

The Color Association

Beautiful colours with cool graphics. CAUS is the oldest colour forecasting service in the US. Since 1915, they have provided colour forecasting information to various industries including those of apparel, accessories, textiles and home furnishings. In addition, assorted industry professionals comment on where they find inspiration and how it influences the direction of colour. You've got to become a member to get information.
www.colorassociation.com

Visual Merchandising and Store Design

A subscription page and industry magazine for visual merchandizers, store planners, architects, designers and interior designers. The information includes latest techniques, technology and trends and design and trade-show coverage updates.
www.vmsd.com

Baal-Teshuva J (2001)
Christo and Jeanne-Claude
Germany: Taschen

Beckwith C and Fisher A (2002)
African Ceremonies
New York: Harry N Abrams, Inc

Black S, ed. (2006)
Fashioning Fabrics:
Contemporary Textiles in Fashion
London: Black Dog Publishing

Bloom: A Horti-Cultural View
(February 2003) Issue 9
France: United Publishers SA

Blossfeldt K (1985)
Art Forms in the Plant World
New York: Dover Publications Inc

Borelli L (2004)
Fashion Illustration Next
London: Thames & Hudson

Brogden J (1971)
Fashion Design
London: Studio Vista

Callaway N, ed. (1988)
Issey Miyake:
Photographs by Irving Penn
Japan: Miyake Design Studio
New York: Callaway Editions Inc

Charles-Roux E (2005)
The World of Coco Chanel:
Friends Fashion Fame
London: Thames & Hudson

Cole D (2003)
1000 Patterns
London: A & C Black Publishers Ltd

Cosgrave B (2005)
Sample: 100 Fashion Designers,
10 Curators
London: Phaidon Press Ltd

Currie N (1994)
Pierre et Gilles
France: Benedikt Taschen

Dawber M (2005)
New Fashion Illustration
London: Batsford Ltd

Diane T and Cassidy T (2005)
Colour Forecasting
Oxford: Blackwell Publishing

Edmaier B (2008)
Earthsong
London: Phaidon Press Ltd

Fukai A (2002)
Fashion:
The Collection of the Kyoto Costume Institute:
A History from the 18th to the 20th Century
Germany: Taschen

Gallienne A and McConnico H (2005)
Colourful World
London: Thames & Hudson

Golbin P and Baron F (2006)
Balenciaga Paris
London: Thames & Hudson

Gooding M (1995)
Patrick Heron (PB Ed.)
London: Phaidon Press Inc

Gorman P (2006)
The Look: Adventures in Rock and Pop Fashion
London: Adelita

Hamann H (2001)
Vertical View
UK: teNeues Publishing Ltd

Hejduk, J and Cook, P (2000)
House of the Book
London: Black Dog Publishing

Hillier J (1992)
Japanese Colour Prints (1st Ed. 1966)
London: Phaidon Press Ltd

Hodge B, Mears P and Sidlauskas S (2006)
Skin + Bones: Parallel Practices in Fashion
and Architecture
London: Thames & Hudson

Holborn M (1995)
Issey Miyake
Germany: Taschen

Itten J (1974)
The Art of Color (1st Ed. 1966)
New York: John Wiley & Sons, Inc

Jenkyn Jones S (2002)
Fashion Design
London: Laurence King Publishing

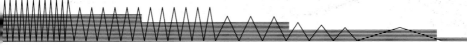

Jiricna E (2001)
Staircases
London: Lawrence King

Joseph-Armstrong H (2000)
Draping for Apparel Design
New York: Fairchild Publications, Inc

Klanten R et al, eds. (2006)
Romantik
Berlin: Die Gestalten Verlag

Klanten R et al, eds. (2004)
Wonderland (2nd Ed.)
Berlin: Die Gestalten Verlag

Knight N and Knapp S (2001)
Flora
New York: Harry N Abrams, Inc

Koda H (2001)
Extreme Beauty: The Body Transformed
New York: The Metropolitan Museum of Art

Koda H (2003)
Goddess: The Classical Mode
New York: Metropolitan Museum of Art

Lauer D (1979)
Design Basics
Holt, Rinehart and Winston

Lawson B (1990)
How Designers Think: The Design Process Demystified (2nd Ed.)
Cambridge: The University Press

Levi-Strauss C, Fukai A and Bloemink B (2005)
Fashion in Colors: Viktor & Rolf & Kci
New York: Editions Assouline

Malin D (2002)
Heaven and Earth: Unseen by the Naked Eye
London: Phaidon Press Ltd

Martin R and Koda H (1995)
Haute Couture
New York: The Metropolitan Museum of Art

McDowell C (2001)
Galliano
London: Weidenfeld & Nicolson

McKelvey K (1996)
Fashion Source Book
Oxford: Blackwell Publishing Ltd

McKelvey K and Munslow J (2003)
**Fashion Design:
Process, Innovation and Practice**
London: Blackwell Publishing Ltd

Nash S and Merkert J (1985)
Naum Gabo: Sixty Years of Constructivism
Prestel-Verlag

Newman C (2001)
National Geographic: Fashion
Washington: National Geographic Society

Parent M, ed. (2000)
Stella
New York: Ipso Facto Publishers

Powell P and Peel L (1988)
'50s & '60s Style
London: The Apple Press Ltd

Sorger R and Udale J (2006)
The Fundamentals of Fashion Design
Switzerland: AVA Publishing SA

Stipelman S (2005)
Illustrating Fashion: Concept to Creation
(2nd Ed.)
New York: Fairchild Publications, Inc.

Tatham C and Seaman J (2003)
Fashion Design Drawing Course
London: Thames & Hudson

**United Colors of Benetton
(Spring/Summer 1999)**
Kokeshi Dolls

Viktor & Rolf, Premiere Decinnie (2003)
Artimo

Wilcox C (2004)
Vivienne Westwood
London: V&A Publications

Wilcox C, ed. (2001)
Radical Fashion
London: V&A Publications

Wilcox C and Mendes V (1998)
Modern Fashion in Detail (1st Ed. 1991)
New York: The Overlook Press

UK Contacts

British Fashion Council
www.londonfashionweek.co.uk
The British Fashion Council owns and organises London Fashion Week and the British Fashion Awards. The BFC has close links with the UK's top fashion design colleges through its Colleges Forum, which acts as an interface between industry and colleges.

Fashion Awareness Direct
www.fad.org.uk
An organization committed to assisting young designers succeed in fashion by bringing students and industry together at introductory events.

Fashion Capital
www.fashioncapital.co.uk
Fashion Capital aims to provide a one-stop online support resource for all areas of the clothing and fashion industry.

Fashion United
www.fashionunited.co.uk
FashionUnited.co.uk is the business-to-business platform for the fashion industry in the UK. It offers all fashion-related websites and information, the latest fashion news and the Fashion Career Centre. The Fashion Career Centre lists current jobs in fashion, gives advice on applying and a free newsletter subscription.

US Contacts

Fashion Information
www.fashioncenter.com

Council of Fashion Designers of America
www.cfda.com

Pantone Color Institute
www.pantone.com

European Contacts

Fashion Awareness Direct (FAD)
www.fad.org.uk
FAD fashion competitions provide young people with opportunities to further their creative and practical skills, integrate cultural research into their work and showcase the results to the industry and media.

Fashion Competitions
London Graduate Fashion Week
www.gfw.org.uk
Graduate Fashion Week was launched in 1991 as a forum to showcase the very best BA graduate fashion design talent in the UK.

Modem
www.modemonline.com
An information resource giving an overview of both fashion and design from the European perspective.

Royal Society for the encouragement of Arts, Manufactures & Commerce
www.thersa.org
The RSA's student annual awards scheme, Design Directions, offers a range of challenging projects that comment on the changing role of the designer in relation to society, technology and culture.

Careers/Work Experience

Contacts Prospects
www.prospects.ac.uk
The careers advice section is an invaluable resource for graduates looking to make the most of their degree and develop their career. Providing comprehensive, in-depth career advice for graduates of any subject, no matter what kind of career guidance you're looking for.

Fabrics and Trims

UK

Broadwick Silks
www.broadwicksilks.com

Cloth House
www.clothhouse.com

Kleins
www.kleins.co.uk

VV Rouleaux
www.vvrouleaux.com

US

M&J Trimming
www.mjtrim.com

NY Elegant Fabrics, NYC
www.nyelegantfabrics.com

Research and Design

Courses

UK

**Central Saint Martins
College of Art and Design**
www.csm.arts.ac.uk

De Montfort University
www.dmu.ac.uk

Kingston University
www.kingston.ac.uk

London College of Fashion
www.fashion.arts.ac.uk

**Manchester Metropolitan
University**
www.artdes.mmu.ac.uk/fashion

Middlesex University
www.mdx.ac.uk

Northbrook College Sussex
www.northbrook.ac.uk

**Northumbria University
School of Design**
www.northumbria.ac.uk

**Ravensbourne College of
Design and Communication**
www.rave.ac.uk

Royal College of Art
www.rca.ac.uk

The Fashion Retail Academy
www.fashionretailacademy.ac.uk

University for the Creative Arts
www.ucreative.ac.uk

University of Brighton
www.brighton.ac.uk

University of Westminster
www.westminster.ac.uk

Europe

Amsterdam Fashion Institute
www.amfi.hva.nl

Domus Academy
www.domusacademy.com

Flanders Fashion Institute
www.ffi.be

**Hogeschool Antwerp,
Fashion Department**
www.antwerp-fashion.be

**Institucion Artistica de
Enseñanza**
www.iade.es

Parsons Paris
www.parsons-paris.com

US

**Fashion Institute of Design and
Merchandising**
www.fidm.com

**Fashion Institute of
Technology**
www.fitnyc.edu

Parsons School of Design
www.parsons.edu

Museums and Galleries

UK

Design Museum
www.designmuseum.org

Fashion and Textiles Museum
www.ftmlondon.org

Fashion Museum Bath
www.museumofcostume.co.uk

Natural History Museum
www.nhm.ac.uk

The British Museum
www.thebritishmuseum.org

The Victoria & Albert Museum
www.vam.ac.uk

Art & Craft Galleries

UK

Barbican
www.barbican.org.uk

**Contemporary Applied
Arts Gallery**
www.caa.org.uk

Royal Academy of Arts
www.royalacademy.org.uk

Tate Modern
www.tate.org.uk/modern

The Crafts Council
www.craftscouncil.org.uk

US

**Cooper-Hewitt, National
Design Museum**
www.cooperhewitt.org

**The Metropolitan Museum
of Art**
www.metmuseum.org

The Museum of Modern Art
www.moma.org

**Solomon R. Guggenheim
Museum**
www.guggenheim.org

**Whitney Museum of
American Art**
www.whitney.org

Europe

Louvre Museum
www.louvre.fr

**ModeMuseum Provincie
Antwerpen – MoMu**
www.momu.be

Musée d'Orsay
www.musee-orsay.fr

Palazzo Pitti Costume Gallery
www.polomuseale.firenze.it

**The Musée de la Mode
et du Textile**
www.lesartsdecoratifs.fr

Triennale di Milano
www.triennale.it

Japan

The Kyoto Costume Institute
www.kci.or.jp

Index

On the writing and production of this second edition I would like to thank all the talented designers, fashion writers, academics, photographers and students who have contributed such amazing work.

In particular, I would like to thank Omar Kashoura, Alice Palmer, Julien Macdonald, Richard Sorger, Wendy Dagworthy, Jenny Packham, Dr.Noki, David Downton, the team at WGSN and Caryn Franklin. To Daniel and Alex at the Royal College of Art, also to Victoria Hicks at Southampton Solent University and the students of Northbrook College Sussex Fashion design degree, past and present, who have supplied much of the new sketchbook content, thank you and good luck with your future careers. Thanks also to Tacita Meredith for her beautiful illustrations on the front cover as well as for her creative sketchbooks.

To Claire Pepper, you continue to be an amazing photographer and I thank you for the images we have retained in this second edition. Also to Nick Sinton for helping to photograph all the many sketchbooks late into the night. And finally to the talents of Chris Moore and Paul Hartnett and to Chi at PYMCA who have supplied amazing street, archive and catwalking photography that have enriched this title throughout.

A big thank you goes to my editor Colette Meacher, especially for those days spent in the office reading through all the endless changes over coffee and chocolates!

To all those at AVA Publishing for helping to make the first edition such a huge success and for allowing me to re-develop the second edition entirely again. Thank you to John McGill for the creative layout and design that has been brought to the second edition and given the book a fantastic new look and feel.

To my Mother and Father for the education they provided me with and the love and support they have always offered. And finally to my dearest partner Gary who has always supported and encouraged me throughout this writing process, I love you. xx

Picture credits
p013 Louisa Payne; p015 Lotta Lindblad; p047 Emma-Jane Lord; p048 Victoria Hicks, Richard Sorger, Rebekah Train; p049 Linda Ramsted, Tacita Meredith; p50 Roxanne Goldstein; p051 Danielle Collier, Joe Goode; p60 Roxanne Goldstein; p067 Tacita Meredith; p082 Rebekah Train and Leigh Gibson; p083 Victoria Hicks; p086 Emma-Jane Lord; p087 Danielle Brindley, Roxanne Goldstein; p090 Danielle Collier; p091 Emma-Jane Lord, Roxanne Goldstein; p092 Danielle Collier; p094 Victoria Hicks; p96 Lara Dumbleton; p097 Joe Goode; p098 Victoria Hicks; p099 Emma Jane Lord, Roxanne Goldstein; p100 Danielle Collier, Gemma Ashe; p101 Joe Goode, Roxanne Goldstein; pp102–3 Victoria Hicks; p112 Rhea Fields; p113 Emma Jane Lord; pp114–5 Sarka Chaloupkova, Rebekah Train; pp116–117 Rhea Fields, Danielle Brindley; p127 Rhea Fields; p128 Roxanne Goldstein; p130 Joe Goode; p142 Danielle Collier; p143 Lara Dumbleton; p144 Roxanne Goldstein, Danielle Collier; p145 Roxanne Goldstein; p154 Steven Dell; p155 Danielle Collier; p158 Louisa Payne; p159 Lotta Lindblad; p160 Joe Goode; p162 Louisa Payne, Gemma Ashe; p163 Rhea Fields; p165 Joe Goode.

BASICS
FASHION DESIGN

Lynne Elvins
Naomi Goulder

Working with ethics

Publisher's note

The subject of ethics is not new, yet its consideration within the applied visual arts is perhaps not as prevalent as it might be. Our aim here is to help a new generation of students, educators and practitioners find a methodology for structuring their thoughts and reflections in this vital area.

AVA Publishing hopes that these **Working with ethics** pages provide a platform for consideration and a flexible method for incorporating ethical concerns in the work of educators, students and professionals. Our approach consists of four parts:

The **introduction** is intended to be an accessible snapshot of the ethical landscape, both in terms of historical development and current dominant themes.

The **framework** positions ethical consideration into four areas and poses questions about the practical implications that might occur. Marking your response to each of these questions on the scale shown will allow your reactions to be further explored by comparison.

The **case study** sets out a real project and then poses some ethical questions for further consideration. This is a focus point for a debate rather than a critical analysis so there are no predetermined right or wrong answers.

A selection of **further reading** for you to consider areas of particular interest in more detail.

Ethical: awareness/ reflection/ debate

Working with ethics

Introduction

Ethics is a complex subject that interlaces the idea of responsibilities to society with a wide range of considerations relevant to the character and happiness of the individual. It concerns virtues of compassion, loyalty and strength, but also of confidence, imagination, humour and optimism. As introduced in ancient Greek philosophy, the fundamental ethical question is: *what should I do?* How we might pursue a 'good' life not only raises moral concerns about the effects of our actions on others, but also personal concerns about our own integrity.

In modern times the most important and controversial questions in ethics have been the moral ones. With growing populations and improvements in mobility and communications, it is not surprising that considerations about how to structure our lives together on the planet should come to the forefront. For visual artists and communicators, it should be no surprise that these considerations will enter into the creative process.

Some ethical considerations are already enshrined in government laws and regulations or in professional codes of conduct. For example, plagiarism and breaches of confidentiality can be punishable offences. Legislation in various nations makes it unlawful to exclude people with disabilities from accessing information or spaces. The trade of ivory as a material has been banned in many countries. In these cases, a clear line has been drawn under what is unacceptable.

But most ethical matters remain open to debate, among experts and lay-people alike, and in the end we have to make our own choices on the basis of our own guiding principles or values. Is it more ethical to work for a charity than for a commercial company? Is it unethical to create something that others find ugly or offensive?

Specific questions such as these may lead to other questions that are more abstract. For example, is it only effects on humans (and what they care about) that are important, or might effects on the natural world require attention too?

Is promoting ethical consequences justified even when it requires ethical sacrifices along the way? Must there be a single unifying theory of ethics (such as the Utilitarian thesis that the right course of action is always the one that leads to the greatest happiness of the greatest number), or might there always be many different ethical values that pull a person in various directions?

As we enter into ethical debate and engage with these dilemmas on a personal and professional level, we may change our views or change our view of others. The real test though is whether, as we reflect on these matters, we change the way we act as well as the way we think. Socrates, the 'father' of philosophy, proposed that people will naturally do 'good' if they know what is right. But this point might only lead us to yet another question: *how do we know what is right*?

You
What are your ethical beliefs?

Central to everything you do will be your attitude to people and issues around you. For some people, their ethics are an active part of the decisions they make every day as a consumer, a voter or a working professional. Others may think about ethics very little and yet this does not automatically make them unethical. Personal beliefs, lifestyle, politics, nationality, religion, gender, class or education can all influence your ethical viewpoint.

Using the scale, where would you place yourself? What do you take into account to make your decision? Compare results with your friends or colleagues.

Your client
What are your terms?

Working relationships are central to whether ethics can be embedded into a project, and your conduct on a day-to-day basis is a demonstration of your professional ethics. The decision with the biggest impact is whom you choose to work with in the first place. Cigarette companies or arms traders are often-cited examples when talking about where a line might be drawn, but rarely are real situations so extreme. At what point might you turn down a project on ethical grounds and how much does the reality of having to earn a living affect your ability to choose?

Using the scale, where would you place a project? How does this compare to your personal ethical level?

01 02 03 04 05 06 07 08 09 10

01 02 03 04 05 06 07 08 09 10

Your specifications
What are the impacts of your materials?

In relatively recent times, we are learning that many natural materials are in short supply. At the same time, we are increasingly aware that some man-made materials can have harmful, long-term effects on people or the planet. How much do you know about the materials that you use? Do you know where they come from, how far they travel and under what conditions they are obtained? When your creation is no longer needed, will it be easy and safe to recycle? Will it disappear without a trace? Are these considerations your responsibility or are they out of your hands?

Using the scale, mark how ethical your material choices are.

Your creation
What is the purpose of your work?

Between you, your colleagues and an agreed brief, what will your creation achieve? What purpose will it have in society and will it make a positive contribution? Should your work result in more than commercial success or industry awards? Might your creation help save lives, educate, protect or inspire? Form and function are two established aspects of judging a creation, but there is little consensus on the obligations of visual artists and communicators toward society, or the role they might have in solving social or environmental problems. If you want recognition for being the creator, how responsible are you for what you create and where might that responsibility end?

Using the scale, mark how ethical the purpose of your work is.

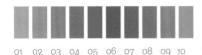

01 02 03 04 05 06 07 08 09 10

01 02 03 04 05 06 07 08 09 10

Working with ethics

One aspect of fashion design that raises an ethical dilemma is the way that clothes production has changed in terms of the speed of delivery of products and the now international chain of suppliers. 'Fast fashion' gives shoppers the latest styles sometimes just weeks after they first appeared on the catwalk, at prices that mean they can wear an outfit once or twice and then replace it. Due to lower labour costs in poorer countries, the vast majority of Western clothes are made in Asia, Africa, South America or Eastern Europe in potentially hostile and sometimes inhumane working conditions. It can be common for one piece of clothing to be made up of components from five or more countries, often thousands of miles apart, before they end up in the high-street store. How much responsibility should a fashion designer have in this situation if manufacture is controlled by retailers and demand is driven by consumers? Even if designers wish to minimise the social impact of fashion, what might they most usefully do?

Traditional Hawaiian feather capes (called *'Ahu'ula*) were made from thousands of tiny bird feathers and were an essential part of aristocratic regalia. Initially they were red (*'Ahu'ula* literally means 'red garment') but yellow feathers, being especially rare, became more highly prized and were introduced to the patterning.

The significance of the patterns, as well as their exact age or place of manufacture is largely unknown, despite great interest in their provenance in more recent times. Hawaii was visited in 1778 by English explorer Captain James Cook and feather capes were amongst the objects taken back to Britain.

The basic patterns are thought to reflect gods or ancestral spirits, family connections and an individual's rank or position in society. The base layer for these garments is a fibre net, with the surface made up of bundles of feathers tied to the net in overlapping rows. Red feathers came from the *'i'iwi* or the *'apapane*. Yellow feathers came from a black bird with yellow tufts under each wing called *'oo'oo*, or a *mamo* with yellow feathers above and below the tail.

Thousands of feathers were used to make a single cape for a high chief (the feather cape of King Kamehameha the Great is said to have been made from the feathers of around 80,000 birds). Only the highest-ranking chiefs had the resources to acquire enough feathers for a full-length cape, whereas most chiefs wore shorter ones which came to the elbow.

The demand for these feathers was so great that they acquired commercial value and provided a full-time job for professional feather-hunters. These fowlers studied the birds and caught them with nets or with bird lime smeared on branches. As both the 'i'iwi and 'apapane were covered with red feathers, the birds were killed and skinned. Other birds were captured at the beginning of the moulting season, when the yellow display feathers were loose and easily removed without damaging the birds.

The royal family of Hawaii eventually abandoned the feather cape as the regalia of rank in favour of military and naval uniforms decorated with braid and gold. The 'oo'oo and the mamo became extinct through the destruction of their forest feeding grounds and imported bird diseases. Silver and gold replaced red and yellow feathers as traded currency and the manufacture of feather capes became a largely forgotten art.

Is it more ethical to create clothing for the masses rather than for a few high-ranking individuals?

Is it unethical to kill animals to make garments?

Would you design and make a feather cape?

Fashion is a form of ugliness so intolerable that we have to alter it every six months.

Oscar Wilde

AIGA
Design Business and Ethics
2007, AIGA

Eaton, Marcia Muelder
Aesthetics and the Good Life
1989, Associated University Press

Ellison, David
Ethics and Aesthetics in European Modernist Literature:
From the Sublime to the Uncanny
2001, Cambridge University Press

Fenner, David E W (Ed)
Ethics and the Arts:
An Anthology
1995, Garland Reference Library of Social Science

Gini, Al and Marcoux, Alexei M
Case Studies in Business Ethics
2005, Prentice Hall

McDonough, William and Braungart, Michael
Cradle to Cradle:
Remaking the Way We Make Things
2002, North Point Press

Papanek, Victor
Design for the Real World:
Making to Measure
1972, Thames & Hudson

United Nations Global Compact
The Ten Principles
www.unglobalcompact.org/AboutTheGC/TheTenPrinciples/index.html